THE SANATANA DHARMA
STUDY GUIDE

SRI DHARMA PRAVARTAKA ACHARYA

THE SANATANA DHARMA STUDY GUIDE

SRI DHARMA PRAVARTAKA ACHARYA

ISDS
OMAHA, NE, USA

2014

iv

International Sanatana Dharma Society
13917 P Street
Omaha, NE 68137

© Copyright 2014, 2016, International Sanatana Dharma Society

www.dharmacentral.com

Works by Sri Dharma Pravartaka Acharya

Sanatana Dharma: The Eternal Natural Way

The Vedic Way of Knowing God

Living Dharma: The Teachings of Sri Dharma Pravartaka Acharya

Radical Universalism: Are All Religions The Same?

Taking Refuge in Dharma: The Initiation Guidebook

The Shakti Principle: Encountering the Feminine Power of God

The Art of Wisdom: Affirmations for Boundless Living

Vedanta: The Culmination of Wisdom

The Dharma Dialogues

The Sanatana Dharma Study Guide

The Encyclopedia of Sanatana Dharma

All these works can be purchased at:

www.dharmacentral.com

Table of Contents

Other Works by Sri Dharma Pravartaka Acharya   v

Table of Contents   vii

Dedication   ix

Introduction   xi

Acknowledgements   xv

First Wave - The Foundations   1

Chapter 1   The Eternal Natural Way   1

Second Wave - Philosophical Grounding   13

Chapter 2   The Philosophical Foundations of Dharma   14

Chapter 3   Epistemology in Literary Form: The Scriptures of Sanatana Dharma   36

Chapter 4   Metaphysics: The Nature of Reality   50

Chapter 5   Ontology: Human Person, God and Creation   57

    A) The Human Person   57

    B) God: The Nature of the Absolute   79

    C) The Material Cosmos   90

Chapter 6   Ethics: Walking the Talk   96

Third Wave - Socio-Historical Grounding   121

Chapter 7   Comparing Religious Traditions   122

Chapter 8   Sanatana Dharma Today   134

Fourth Wave - Grounding in Practice   141

Chapter 9   Taking Refuge in Dharma   142

Chapter 10   Dharma in Practice   156

Chapter 11   Living Dharma Today   196

Chapter 12   Resources   200

Quizzes   209

Appendix - Sanatana Dharma by the Numbers   233
Glossary   235
Bibliography - Primary Sources   247
Bibliography - Secondary Sources   253
About the Author   257

Dedication

The present work is dedicated to Śrī Narada Muni,
my *shiksha guru*, the foremost of all *rishis* (seer-sages),
the greatest Vishva Guru (teacher of the universe),
and the preeminent philosopher of Bhakti Yoga.
May his teachings and example always guide the work of
the International Sanatana Dharma Society.

ॐ नमो नारायणाय

Introduction

The Sanatana Dharma Study Guide was written with the purpose of helping readers to more fully grasp the teachings contained in another book that I have previously written titled *Sanatana Dharma: The Eternal Natural Way*. Thus, *The Sanatana Dharma Study Guide* is somewhat akin to the proverbial finger pointing to Truth. While the finger, too, has value, its purpose is to help steer the sincere spiritual seeker to something higher than itself. *Sanatana Dharma: The Eternal Natural Way* is the most comprehensive and philosophically accurate accounting of the ancient path of Vedic spirituality ever written. *Sanatana Dharma: The Eternal Natural Way* was designed to help its readers more deeply understand the ancient spiritual tradition that known as Sanatana Dharma. This tradition has also been known by several other names and terms in the past. Some have referred to this tradition as "the Vedic tradition", or "Yoga spirituality", or as "Hinduism". What the tradition truly is, however, is more fully known as Sanatana Dharma, which can be translated into English as "the Eternal Natural Way."

Sanatana Dharma is the most ancient spiritual tradition on Earth. It is a spiritual tradition that transcends any form of denominationalism, sectarianism, fanaticism or blind faith. This is the case because its source is not anything earthly or man-made. Rather, Sanatana Dharma is the Eternal Natural Law that has God alone as its transcendental source, and that serves as the foundational ordering principle of all reality, including the natural ordering principles of all properly functioning human societies. If we can somehow or other understand the deepest essence of what Sanatana Dharma has to offer us, and learn how to apply those teachings in our own lives, we can then know that highest Truth that will reveal to us the happiness, the positive growth, the fearlessness, the healthy well-being, and the wisdom that we have been searching for all of our lives.

To truly understand Sanatana Dharma in the purest and most authentic way, however, is not the easiest of tasks. Indeed, even many of those who have been on the path of Sanatana Dharma for many years sometimes have difficulty fully understanding this tradition on its own terms. The difficulty that so many modern practitioners of Vedic and Yoga spirituality have in fully understanding their own tradition is brought about because of several factors.

One of these is the fact that this tradition offers us a world-view and a philosophical system that is the most detailed, comprehensive and holistic approach to understanding reality that exists in our world. Sanatana Dharma offers us a seemingly endless universe of sacred texts that delve deeply into many aspects of spiritual culture, philosophy, arts and sciences. It offers us a depth of explanation that is not found in any other religious tradition, collection of literature, or world-view that exists. What Sanatana Dharma offers us is spiritual depth and authenticity. Sadly, these are values that our post-modern, crass consumerist culture no longer holds in the highest of esteem. Thus, Sanatana Dharma can only be fully known by the few who are willing to devote the time to truly understand it.

If your approach to spiritual enquiry is to try to receive a supposed "truth" that is quick, simplistic, faddish, and based upon passing sentiment rather than thoughtful reflection - then Sanatana Dharma is not the spiritual tradition for you! But if you are seeking a path that truly offers answers to every important philosophical, cosmological, ontological and metaphysical question that you can think to ask, then Sanatana Dharma will satisfy your queries completely and without any omission. Sanatana Dharma is not just a feel-good, New Age escape. It is a vast spiritual culture, civilization, and world-view.

Another reason why some have struggled to fully grasp the greatness of Vedic teachings is due to the esoteric nature of how truth is conveyed by the tradition. Sanatana Dharma is not a do-it-yourself exercise, as many attempts at spirituality now are in the modern West. It is not something that we can ever fully teach ourselves. Rather, its deepest truths can only be revealed to us by someone who has himself penetrated those mysteries, experienced firsthand the liberating results of such spiritual discovery, and has been empowered directly by the Infinite Divine to then convey that truth to others. In other words, without the benefit of a living and qualified *guru*, it is practically impossible to fully understand what the Vedic scriptures are trying to convey.

My book, *Sanatana Dharma: The Eternal Natural Way*, was specifically designed to address both of these problems, and to convey the full extent of the Vedic tradition in a way that is both complete in its treatment of the subject, as well as accessible in a living and experiential way to the modern Vedic spiritual practitioner. *The Sanatana Dharma Study Guide* is meant to be a companion text to my main introductory work *Sanatana Dharma: The Eternal Natural Way*. Therefore, ideally, both books should be studied together. If a person does not have a copy of *Sanatana Dharma: The Eternal Natural Way*, however, then the present book can also work as a stand-alone text to help gain a good introductory understanding of the tradition of Sanatana Dharma.

How To Use This Book

The book is formatted in a way to help support and deepen your understanding of *Sanatana Dharma: The Eternal Natural Way*. Therefore, it provides a brief and easy way to understand summation of each section of the book. It also provides many scriptural references supporting the philosophical teachings that are presented in each section the book. There are also many exercises, questions, contemplations and other activities that are assigned to each section. At the end of the book is a series of twenty quizzes that can be answered either by the individual reader, or in a group setting. This book is designed to be helpful when used either by individual readers, or by study groups dedicated to discussing the book *Sanatana Dharma: The Eternal Natural Way* in a more formal group setting.

However you choose to use *The Sanatana Dharma Study Guide*, it is my sincere hope that this book will help facilitate the deepening of your understanding and practice of Vedic spirituality.

Aum Tat Sat

Sri Dharma Pravartaka Acharya
International Sanatana Dharma Society
December 15, 2014
Omaha, Nebraska, USA
www.dharmacentral.com

Acknowledgements

There are many people who have supported and encouraged my work over the decades who I owe an enormous and sincere debt of gratitude to. While this list is not at all complete, it is at least a small attempt to offer acknowledgement to some of the people who I must thank. May my small offering of thanks please them all.

My spiritual teachers: Sri Narada Muni, Sri Ramanuja Acharya, Sri B. R. Sridhara Swami, Sri Bhaktivedanta Swami Prabhupada, Sri Swami Jyotirmayananda, Sri Tirumalai Krishnamacharya, Pujya Sri Swami Dayananda Sarasvati, Dr. David Frawley (Sri Acharya Vamadeva Shastri), Sri Pandurang Shastri Athavale.

My early Yoga *asana* teachers: Sri Dharma Mittra and Sri Swami Bua.

My colleagues, friends and supporters: Paramacharya Palaniswami of *Hinduism Today Magazine,* Dr. Keith Yandell, Dr. David M. Knipe, Dr. Klaus Klostermeier, Dr. Robert Thurman, Dr. Georg Fueurstein, Dr. Subhash Kak, Dr. Deepak Chopra, Sri Swami Nirbhayananda, Sri Swami Sivadasa Bharati, Sri Vishal Agarwal, Dr. Subhash Kak, Sri Vrindavan Parker, Stephen Knapp, Yogi Baba Prem, B.A. Paramadwaiti Swami.

To all of my disciples, without whose tremendous encouragement, support, trust and love I could have accomplished little.

My special thanks are offered to Tulasi Devi for her brilliant layout and design, as well as the beautiful cover art of this book – and all of my books. Her amazing creativity and aesthetic expertise made the creation of this book possible.

First Wave - The Foundations

Sanatana Dharma: The Eternal Natural Way is divided into four separate sections that I have called Waves. This is in keeping with the Sanskrit name of this work, *Sanatana-Dharma-Amrita-Sindhu*, or "The Nectarian Ocean of the Eternal Natural Way." The First Wave of this great ocean of eternal truths lays out the foundational elements of the Vedic tradition, including establishing the uniqueness of Sanatana Dharma, discussing some of the more important facts and figures of the tradition, and a quick philosophical overview to give readers a foundation for their understanding of the rest of the book.

Chapter 1   The Eternal Natural Way

1.1.1 The Two Approaches to Our Cosmos

There are two fundamental ways in which any thinking person can choose to view the meaning of life and of our universe around us. These two different ways are 1) that the universe we are living in is ultimately a meaningless and empty reality, full of disorder and chaos, or 2) that the reality we find ourselves in does have inherent meaning and purpose, even if initially somewhat of a mystery to us, and that this deep meaning can be known and positively applied in our lives. The latter approach to life and our cosmos is the most healthy view to take, and is an expression of Sanatana Dharma.

"The afterlife never rises before the eyes of the immature person, deluded by the delusion of wealth. 'This is the world', he thinks, 'there is no other'; thus he falls again and again under my Death's sway. (*Katha Upanishad*, 1:2.6)

"Childish fools pursue external desires and enter the wide chords of death. The sages, having comprehended the liberated condition, never pray for the temporary things of this world." (*Katha Upanishad*, 4.2)

> Question: Can you remember instances in your life in which you clearly felt the loving order of the universe operating in your life?

> Exercise: Try daily to increasingly discern the hidden meaning behind the universe by contemplating nature, the scriptures and the teachings of the *guru*.

1.1.2 Normative Religion Versus Sanatana Dharma

The normative approach to religion is to see religion in terms of denominationalism, the idea that there are multiple religions, each of which is the institutionalization of a man-made (*paurusheya*) opinion on the nature of our reality and our place within that reality. Sanatana Dharma, on the other hand, is not normative in this sense since it transcends temporal, organizational institutions, man-made opinions, and even religion itself. Rather, Sanatana Dharma is an organic expression of the spirituality of the cosmos itself. It is not man-made, but an eternal reflection of Truth.

Additionally, pure and unadulterated Sanatana Dharma is not to be confused with the more modern denomination known as "Hinduism". While modern "Hinduism" is an outgrowth of Sanatana Dharma (as all reli-

gions are, either directly or indirectly), and is perhaps the closest in like-
ness to Sanatana Dharma of all the religions in existence today, Sanatana
Dharma is the unaltered tradition of Vedic spirituality that pre-existed
even modern "Hinduism". Followers of authentic Vedic spirituality,
therefore, reject the modern term "Hinduism" and embrace, instead, the
true and original name of our path, which is: Sanatana Dharma. The term
for a follower of Sanatana Dharma is a Dharmi.

*Satyam bruyatpriyam bruyann bruyat satyam priyam
priyam cha nanrtam bruyadesha dharmah sanatanah*

"Let him speak that which is true. Let him say what is pleasing. Let him
utter no disagreeable truth, and let him utter no agreeable falsehood
merely to please another. That is essence of the eternal natural law (*dharmah sanatanah*)." (*Manava Dharma Shastra*, 4.138)

"Considering religion to be observance of rituals and performance of
acts of charity, the deluded remain ignorant of the highest good. Having
enjoyed in heaven the reward of their good works, they enter again into
the world of mortals." (*Mundaka Upanishad*, 1:2:10)

Questions: What were some of the experiences you had with
man-made, denominational religion versus your experiences with
the Eternal Natural Way? What is God's sect or denomination?

Exercise: Each day, align your mind and activities increasingly
with the Eternal Natural Way, and not with sectarianism.

1.1.3 Uniqueness of Sanatana Dharma

Though various religions share many things in common, religions are neither all the same, nor are they all equal.[1] Religions are often very different in their goals and in their means toward their respective goals. Sanatana Dharma is unlike any other religion in several unique ways. As only a few examples, ours is the only spiritual tradition that does not have a time of founding anywhere in human history. We cannot say that Sanatana Dharma was "founded" at x time in human history. Also, unlike other religious traditions, we do not have a specific human founder. Sanatana means "eternal". Thus, our path transcends time. We cannot say that it was ever created in the same way as all the other religions on Earth were created as one time or another.

"Truth alone prevails, not falsehood. By truth the path is laid out, the way of the gods, on which the seers, whose every desire is satisfied, proceed to the highest abode of the True." (*Mundaka Upanishad*, 3.1.6)

"Never was there a time when I did not exist, nor you, nor all of these kings. Nor in the future shall any of us cease to be." (*Bhagavad Gita*, 2.12)

> Questions: Who are the founders, and what were the dates of founding, of some of the other world religions? What does it mean for something to have never been founded? Having never been founded, is it really possible for Sanatana Dharma to ever disappear?

---

[1] For further information on the meaning of religious differences, please read my book *Radical Universalism: Are All Religions The Same?*

1.1.4 The Vedic Revelation

Here we deal with the nature of Shastra, or the Vedic scriptures. All of Sanatana Dharma is based upon the revealed teachings of the Vedic scriptures. It is precisely because our path is predicated upon the *Vedas* that it is also sometimes called Vedic spirituality, or the Vedic tradition. *Veda* means literally "knowledge" and includes all the many scriptures of Sanatana Dharma. Indeed, the Vedic literature is vast, with many different sub-genres of literatures.

The reason why there are so many sacred books in the Vedic canon is because these works deal not only with spirituality and philosophy, but also with every other single aspect of the human experience: science, mathematics, health and medicine, art and culture, music and dance, martial arts, culinary arts, architecture, city planning, astrophysics, astrology, history, etc. The Vedic scriptures examine and explain these many different fields from a transcendental perspective. Though it can seem daunting that there is such a massive collection of scriptures available to us in the Vedic revelation, the gist and essence of the most important teachings of all the Vedic literatures are summarized expertly for us in the form of the *Bhagavad Gita*.

"The Yamadutas stated: That which is prescribed in the Vedic scriptures constitutes Dharma, the Natural Law. The opposite of what is prescribed in the *Vedas* is *adharma*, or the path of unrighteousness. The Vedic scriptures are directly the Supreme Godhead, Narayana, and are self-born. This we have heard from Yamaraja." (*Srimad Bhagavatam*, 6.1.40)

Questions: What Vedic scriptures have you read so far? What scriptures do you want to read next? What topics are you interested in? There is somewhere in the Vedic scriptures where that topic is discussed!

Exercise: As you read through the *Bhagavad Gita* or some other Vedic scripture, do so as a meditation, reading it slowly, only a few passages at a time, and allowing its teachings to resonate deeply within your heart. To know the full meaning of the scriptures, you must consult either with a *guru* or the *guru's* representative.

1.1.5 Who is a Dharmi?

The question of who has the ability and right to call themselves a Dharmi, or a follower of Sanatana Dharma, is a very important one. This is the case because it is not possible to fully practice a spiritual path unless one fully identifies with, and has fidelity to, that path. Identity gives us strength and confidence in our practice.

Being a follower of Sanatana Dharma is not determined by being "born" into the religion, or by any other external or physical factor. Rather, the only factor that makes that determination is a purely internal one. It is one of *shraddha*, or healthy faith. If one accepts the scriptures of Sanatana Dharma as his guide in life, if one accepts the teachings of Sanatana Dharma, and if he openly acknowledges Sanatana Dharma as his religious path, then one is a follower of Sanatana Dharma. A Dharmi is any person who accepts Sanatana Dharma as their path toward Truth.

Sanatana Dharma is a path that is open to all people, regardless of their race, nationality, ethnicity, language, 'caste', gender, sexual orientation or any other material factor. While individual Hindus have certainly been guilty of prejudice in the past, as is true of members of all other religions, authentic Sanatana Dharma as a spiritual tradition has never advocated persecution of others due merely to differences in body, opinion, religion or ideology. It never will. All are welcomed into the universal family of Dharma in accordance with only one standard: they must be sincere and they must have a good heart.

"In accordance with each person's individual disposition, he will acquire a particular type of faith. This human being is comprised of faith. As his faith, so is he." (*Bhagavad Gita*, 17.3)

> Questions: What form or path did your own personal journey to Dharma take? If you were "born" in the Vedic tradition, how well do you understand our tradition and how much do you practice it in daily life?

1.1.6 Monotheistic Panentheism

Sanatana Dharma teaches that there is ultimately one, supreme and indivisible Absolute who is the source and meaning of all reality. This Absolute possesses infinite auspicious attributes. In this sense, then, Sanatana Dharma is a monotheistic religion. It does not, however, subscribe to the form of monotheism that is practiced by the Abrahamic religions (Judaism, Christianity and Islam), which is what is called Anthropomorphic Monotheism (i.e., the notion that the Supreme has very human-like attributes). Rather, we follow Panentheistic[2] Monotheism, which is the teaching that God is both fully transcendent and fully imminent in all things around us. God is the transcendental source of all reality. But He is also present in everything that exists. More, God is not made in our

---

[2] Pan*en*theism is not to be confused with pantheism.

image (anthropomorphism), but we are made in God's divine image (theomorphism).

Ekam evadvitiyam

"He is One only without a second." (*Chandogya Upanishad*, 6:2:1)

Na chasya kaschij janita na chadhipah

"The One has no master in this world, no ruler, nor are there any signs of the One. The One is the cause, the cause of all the causes. The One has no progenitor nor controller." (*Shvetashvatara Upanishad*, 6:9)

"The Supreme Godhead is Himself this cosmos, and still He is aloof from it. From Him only has this cosmic manifestation emanated, in Him it rests, and unto Him it enters after annihilation." (*Srimad Bhagavatam*, 1.5.20)

"That Brahman (God) shines forth, vast, self-luminous, inconceivable, subtler than the subtle. He is far beyond what is far, and yet here very near at hand. Verily, He is seen here, dwelling in the cave of the heart of conscious beings." (*Mundaka Upanishad*, 3.1.7)

"Narayana is the Supreme Reality designated as Brahman. Narayana is the highest. Narayana is the supreme Light (described in the *Upanishads*). Narayana is the infinite Supreme Self." (*Maha-Narayana Upanishad*, 13:4)

"Whatsoever there is in this world known through perception (because of their proximity) or known through report (because of their distance), all that is pervaded by Narayana within and without." (*Maha-Narayana Upanishad*, 13:5)

"All the demigods and all the philosophers who desire liberation bow down to the Supreme Godhead." (*Narsimha-Tapani Upanishad*, *Purva Khanda* 2.4)

"The pure devotee is always within the core of My heart, and I am always in the heart of the pure devotee. My devotees do not know anything else but Me, and I do not know anyone else but them." (*Srimad Bhagavatam*, 9.4.68)

Questions: What were some of your earliest memories of trying to imagine what God was like? What about now?

Contemplation: There is never a time in which we are ever truly separated from God. What we sometimes suffer from is only the illusion of separation.

1.1.7 Vishva Dharma: The Universal Path

Sanatana Dharma is not the religion of any one nation, people or ethnic group. It is not even the religion of only one particular planet or universe. Rather, Sanatana Dharma is open to all sincere seekers. Any person who sincerely accepts Sanatana Dharma as his own religion is consequently a follower of this path. In this way, Sanatana Dharma is the universal path for all sincere and good beings.

Vasudhaiva Kutumbakam

"The world is but one family." (*Mahopanishad* VI.71)

Question: What is the difference between Vedic Universalism versus Radical Universalism?

Fact: There are multiple universes, and Dharma is the operative principle in all of them.

1.1.8 Ethnicity Versus Religion

Ethnicity and religion is not the same thing. Ethnicity is determined by one's genetic inheritance, which is a DNA driven and physical factor. We are born with an ethnicity. Our ethnicity is, therefore, not a matter of personal choice for an individual. Religion, on the other hand, is completely determined by one's own free will. We are not born with a religious belief. A newborn baby does not have a philosophical or theological belief. We ultimately choose at some point in our lives to adhere to one spiritual/philosophical construct or another, even if we, simply by default, choose to ultimately accept our parents' specific religion as our own. We are still choosing. Religion is, therefore, purely a matter of individual choice, free will and liberty.

"The *atman* is not born, nor does he die; he did not spring from anything, and nothing sprang from him; unborn, eternal, everlasting, ancient, he is not slain although the body is slain." (*Katha Upanishad*, 1.2.18)

> Questions: What was your religion before practicing Sanatana Dharma? Do you know anyone who was born into a different religion before choosing to follow Sanatana Dharma? What is your ethnicity? Did you choose that ethnicity?

1.1.9 Sanatana Dharma is not an "Indian" Religion

All too many people, practitioners and scholars alike, tend to equate Sanatana Dharma with the nation-state of India. The two, however, really have nothing to do with one another. It is true that the majority of people in India today are still followers of Sanatana Dharma, as is also the case for the nations of Nepal, Guyana and Trinidad & Tobago, all of which have majority "Hindu" populations. However, at one time in ancient history, most of the world followed the Vedic path, and not just "India". More, today there are citizens of every nation on Earth who follow Sanatana Dharma. There are European Dharmis, American Dharmis, Russian Dharmis, Japanese Dharmis, Arab Dharmis, etc. Sanatana Dharma is, therefore, not Indian, Asian or Eastern. Rather, it is a path that is, and always has been, practiced universally.

"One does not incur any demerit in neglecting a *'brahmana'* who does not possess Vedic learning, just as one does not pour oblations into ash ignoring a blazing fire." (*Vashishtha Dharma Sutra*, 3.10)

> <u>Contemplation</u>: What determines whether or not a person is a true follower of Dharma is not their national background, "caste" or other bodily consideration. A Dharmi is one who understands and practices Dharma.

1.1.10 The Ancient Dharmic Cultural Sphere

Dharma was at one time (previous to the arising of the Abrahamic faiths) the predominant spiritual world-view on Earth. Though known by many different names in accordance with the specific local language in question, the concept of Natural Law (which is synonymous with Dharma) was the foundation upon which all ancient civilizations were built. Thus, we include among the followers of Dharma everyone who follows any of the pre-Christian European religions (such as Asatru, Druid, Slavic, Greco-Roman, etc.), as well as Zoroastrianism, Taoism, Shinto, etc.

ekam sad vipra bahudha vadanti

"Truth is one, despite the fact that sages call it by various names." (*Rig Veda Samhita*, 1.164.46)

Sam gacchadvam sam vadadhvam
sam no manaamsi jaanataam
Devaa bhaagam yathaa poorve
sam jaanaanaa upaasate

"Together shall we walk, together talk, together our minds understand; Thus did the gods in ancient times reach their divine ends." (*Rig Veda Samhita*, 10.191.2)

> Question: What are some of the cultural or spiritual elements of your own ancient (pre-Abrahamic) cultural heritage that are almost the same as those found in Vedic civilization?

1.1.11 The Dharmi Population

There are followers of Sanatana Dharma all throughout the globe. The total for the whole world is approximately one billion, with roughly five million living in America. Of those living in America, about 2/5 are of South Asian descent (which includes India), and the rest (3/5) are of non-South Asian ethnic ancestry. So, in America for example, the majority of followers of Sanatana Dharma do not trace their ethnic roots back to South Asia (which includes India).

"May the Earth Goddess (Prithvi Devi), who contains upon her people who speak various languages, and who have various *dharmas* according to their own nations of abode, pour upon me a treasure in a thousand streams, like a constant cow that never fails." (*Atharva Veda*, 12.1.45)

Second Wave - Philosophical Grounding

The Second Wave of *Sanatana-dharma-amrita-sindhu*,[3] or "The Nectarian Ocean of the Eternal Natural Way", is one of the largest and most important of the four sections of the book. It focuses on the philosophical foundations of Sanatana Dharma. The most basic of these foundations is what is called Tri-tattva, or the Three Reals that constitute the three most important elements of reality. Thus, a great deal of attention is especially paid to explaining this very important Vedantic concept.

> Guidance: There are several general disciplines that philosophy includes, all of which are spoken about throughout *Sanatana Dharma: The Eternal Natural Way*. These different aspects of philosophy include:
>
> A) **Epistemology**: How it is that knowledge is derived.
> B) **Metaphysics**: Discussions of topics and issues that are beyond the physical realm.
> C) **Ontology**: Different categories of being and substance.
> D) **Cosmology**: Issues pertaining to how the material universe functions.
> E) **Ethics**: The various theories and issues concerning how human beings should behave with one another in order to act in beneficent ways, and not in maleficent ways.

> Fact: The Greek term *philo sophia* means "love of wisdom." The Sanskrit word for "philosophy" is *darshana*, which means both "philosophy" and "to see".

---

[3] This is the Sanskrit name for my book "*Sanatana Dharma: The Eternal Natural Way*".

Chapter 2 The Philosophical Foundations of Sanatana Dharma

2.1.1 Dharma as a World-view

In this section, the history and nature of world-views are touched upon with the goal of establishing that Dharma is not merely a religion, but a world-view, and a fundamental history transforming and civilization transforming idea. Dharma has been an idea that has been as earth-changing as were the much later ideas of monotheism, democracy, the scientific method, or any other way of perceiving the world that have been responsible for tremendous global change. We also begin in this section to explore the full meaning of the term "*sanatana*" as the first part of the dual-compound "*sanatana-dharma*".

> *Dharmo visvasya jagatah pratistha*
> *loke dharmistha prajaupasarpanti*
> *dharmena papamapanudati*
> *dharme sarvam pratisthitam*
> *tasmaddharmam paramam vadanti*

"Dharma constitutes the foundation of all affairs in the world. People respect those who adhere to Dharma. Dharma insulates one against aberrant thoughts. Everything in this world is founded on Dharma. Dharma, therefore, is considered supreme." (*Maha-Narayana Upanishad*, 79.7)

> Questions: If something is eternal, does this simply mean that it will never end in the future? If something is truly eternal, does this not also mean that there was never a time when it did not exist in the past?

2.1.2 Understanding the Concept of Dharma

Here, we continue our exploration of the term "*sanatana-dharma*" by beginning to examine the vast ocean of meaning connected to the word "*dharma*". Dharma denotes the inherent quality of a thing. Dharma is that inner quality that makes any particular thing what it is. Dharma is what makes water wet, and what makes fire hot. On the macrocosmic scale, Dharma means the Natural Law of the entire Cosmos, the inner essence of the Cosmos.

"Dharma sustains society. Dharma maintains the social order. Dharma ensures the well-being and progress of humanity. Dharma is surely that which fulfills these objectives." (*Mahabharata*, *Karna Parva*, 69.58)

> Questions: Can you name the inner essence, or *dharma*, of several individual things? For example, what is the *dharma* of a knife, of space, of time, of a nation's leader, of your own self?

2.1.3 Dharma as Axiomatic

Dharma is not subject to opinion, belief or sect. It is not just a religious term, but also a term that is describing laws of nature that are inexorable and unalterable. The existence and the laws of Dharma are as objective and universally applicable as are the laws of mathematics or physics.

> Question: If someone is of the opinion that $1+1=17$, or that his brother is a married bachelor, or that a perfect circle can be a round square, does merely stating these opinions make them actually true? Unalterable laws are not subject to human opinion.

2.1.4 Dharma as Universally Applicable

Dharma applies to all people at all times and in all circumstances. Dharma is universal in that it was recognized by all the ancient civilizations of the Earth, even if it was called by many different names by those different civilizations. There is a word describing the exact same concept of Dharma in all the languages of every ancient people in the world.

"It is most difficult to define Dharma. Dharma has been explained to be that which helps the upliftment of living beings. Therefore, that which ensures the welfare of living beings is surely Dharma. The learned *rishis* have declared that which sustains is Dharma." (*Mahabharata, Shantiparva,* 109.9-11)

Fact: A few names for Dharma in various languages:

Pali:	Dhamma
Chinese:	Tao
Japanese:	Do/To
Persian:	Asha
Egyptian:	Ma'at
Greek:	Physis
Latin:	Liga Natura
Lithuanian:	Darna

Question: What is the term for Dharma (or Natural Law) in your ethnic language?

2.1.5 Universal Elements of Dharmic Civilizations

There is a unique Dharmic ethos that has been observed to be shared by every society that upholds Dharmic principles. In this section, we discuss a few of the more important behavioral and attitudinal aspects of Dharma that were maintained by all ancient civilizations that respected Dharma. These universal elements of Dharma are only a few of the principles that constitute true civilization.

"Consumption of food, sleeping, fear and sexual enjoyment are the common attributes of both humans and animals. But the special attribute of humans is the ability to acknowledge the principles of Dharma. Bereft of Dharma, a person is no better than the animals." (*Hitopadesha*, 25)

> Question: Can you add to the list of similarities between the ancient Dharma-inspired nations and peoples that is outlined in the book *Sanatana Dharma: The Eternal Natural Way*?

2.1.6 The Logic of Dharma

Dharma, Yoga and other aspects of Vedic spirituality are all too often confused as being some form of unintelligible mystical occultism, or else a form of 1960s style New Age musings. These are all offensive stereotypes, and nothing could be further from the truth. Dharma is certainly a system of spiritual thought and practice that is designed to lead the practitioner toward a transcendent reality. However, Dharma is not illogical, unintelligent, or in any way irrational. On the contrary, Dharma philosophy is based upon some of the most rigid and effective principles of logic, ontology and epistemology ever presented to the world. Vedic spirituality offers people a path that perfectly blends both spiritual experience and intellectual rigor. The very highest culmination of Vedic philosophy (and, thus, of all philosophy) is what is called Vedanta, or "the culmination of wisdom".

"Supreme auspiciousness is attained by the knowledge of the true nature of sixteen categories. These are: the means of valid knowledge (*pramana*), the object of valid knowledge (*prameya*), doubt (*samshaya*), purpose (*prayojana*), familiar instance (*drishtanta*), established conclusion (*siddhanta*), constituent limbs (*avayava*), confutation (*tarka*), ascertainment (*nirnaya*), theoretical discussion (*vada*), wrangling (*jalpa*), petty objections (*vitanda*), fallacy (*hetvabhasa*), quibble (*chala*), futility (*jati*), and occasion for rebuke (*nigrahasthana*)." (*Nyaya Sutras*, 1.1.1)

> Question: How many Vedic schools of philosophy can you name?

> Exercise: Read *"The Vedic Way of Knowing God"* to begin your study of Vedic epistemology,[4] which is considered the beginning of philosophical inquiry.

2.1.7 Dharma as Replicable

While healthy faith is a very important element to cultivate on the spiritual path, blind faith is never a healthy thing to have, and is discouraged in Sanatana Dharma. We do not have assurance in the efficacy of Vedic spirituality merely due to faith alone, but due to the fact that it works! In science, for example, the way that we know that a proposed cause has a definite effect is that the cause/effect sequence is replicable. In other words, anyone who tries to bring about the same effect will be able to do so.

In the same way, we know that such practices of Sanatana Dharma as Yoga, meditation, *pranayama*, etc., work because when we practice these

---

[4] Epistemology is the study of how human beings acquire knowledge and theory of perception.

disciplines under the guidance of an authentic and qualified *guru*, we see that the effect is always reliable. We see with our own experience that the path of Yoga and Dharma works! Such experience then produces a healthy faith that is based upon *sattva-guna*, or the mode of goodness.

"The Supreme Godhead said: Now hear about this. According to the modes of nature acquired by the embodied soul, one's faith can be of three kinds - in goodness, in passion or in ignorance." (*Bhagavad Gita*, 17.2)

> Question: What experiences have you had in your own *sadhana* practice in meditation or Yoga that have increased your healthy faith in the path of Sanatana Dharma?

2.1.8 Dharma as Scientific

There has been an unrelenting war in the Western world between science and religion that has now endured for several hundred years. This war has been unnecessary since there is actually no real conflict between science and religion. Both disciplines seek to uncover truths about the cosmos in which we live. Science's exclusive domain is the empirical realm, the world of material sense objects. Science does not have the ability to comment on anything that is outside of the material senses. Those things that can be detected by the senses form the concrete limit beyond which science cannot pass. The domain of spirituality, on the other hand, is that reality that lies outside the bounds of the senses and the intellect. Both science and spirituality are necessary disciplines if we are going to have a balanced and integral understanding of our reality. Due to this harmonious understanding, Dharma not only sees itself as

20

being naturally allied with science, but as being non-different from science.

"The working senses are superior to dull matter; mind is higher than the senses; intelligence is still higher than the mind; and consciousness is even higher than the intelligence." (*Bhagavad Gita*, 3.42)

> Fact: There are ancient Vedic sciences that cover every field of scientific endeavor. There are Vedic mathematics, Vedic physics, Vedic biology and health sciences, Vedic engineering, and Vedic astronomy, to mention only a few.

2.1.9 The Metaphysical Principles of Dharma

All too often, people will speak about Dharma in the most general sense of being simply the law of nature. But what, precisely, are some of the details of these natural laws? What do these natural laws look like, and how do they operate? In this section, we explore some of the many specific principles of Dharma.

> *Na mutra hi saha yartham pita mata ca tishthatah*
> *na pputradaram na jnati dharmostishthati kevalah*

"When one departs from this world to the next realm, neither father nor mother, neither son nor wife will accompany him. Only the Dharma practiced by an individual accompanies him even after death." (*Manava Dharma Shastra*, 4.239)

1. **Omnisentiency**

This is the principle that assures that life is found everywhere in existence. There is no realm, no universe and no planet that does not have some form of life. More, omnisentiency explains that even many objects that we very often do not associate with being alive actually are alive! Planets (including our Mother Earth), rivers, forests and even mountains all have *atmans*, or eternal souls. They are all alive, even if is it a form of life that we may not be able to immediately comprehend.

2. **Theocentricity**

Theocentricity teaches us that God is both present within, and is the ultimate meaning of, everything in existence. All things have their source, as well as their sustenance and their final destination, in God. God is everything.

3. **Sufficient Causality**

This Dharmic metaphysical principle teaches us that every existent thing in the material world exists in a relationship of cause and effect with other things. There is nothing that does not have a cause. There is also no cause that is not itself an effect of some other cause. When we trace back the sequence of cause and effect, cause and effect to the final source, what we finally discover is God, that being who is the cause of all causes (*karana-karanam*), but which Himself has no cause.

4. **Divine Procession**

Our sojourn in the material world consists of three stages that, together, form a circle. The concept of Divine Procession describes these three stages as a) our origination in the spiritual realm, b) our present state of being in illusion in the material realm, and finally c) our eventually becoming reunited with the spiritual realm for eternity.

"This is the truth: As, from a blazing fire, sparks essentially akin to it fly forth by the thousands, so also, my good friend, do various beings come forth from the imperishable Brahman and unto Him again return." (*Mundaka Upanishad*, 2.1.1)

5. **Primacy of Free Volition**

One of the most essential attributes of our true selves (*atman*) is that we have free will. Without free will, we would not even be conscious, sentient beings. That free will can be used in cooperation with our natural state of surrender to the Divine, or it can be misused in order to create an artificial identity, thus commencing our downward fall into illusion (*maya*). Since free will is an essential aspect of who we are as eternal spiritual beings, we cannot avoid exercising it. But we can do our best to use it for our benefit rather than our harm.

6. **Qualitative Hierarchy**

Every single person and thing in existence is naturally established in its proper place along the vast spectrum of the qualitative hierarchy in relation to every other existing person and thing. No two things, or people, in existence are equal or the same. Everything can be seen as naturally belonging somewhere in the natural hierarchy. Hierarchy is inseparable from Nature.

7. Precedence of Personhood over Individualism

Each and every person is inherently unique. No two people are the same. This principle of Dharma is in keeping with the infinite diversification that springs from God's boundless creativity. Modern individualism reduces the uniqueness of persons to an atomized, amorphous mass, in which there is no distinction from one person to another, and each person's unique beauty of being is sacrificed at the altar of radical egalitarianism. Sanatana Dharma celebrates qualitative personhood, not dehumanizing quantitative individualism. We are eternally persons.

8. Cyclicality of Space/Time/Historical Trends

The Abrahamic (Judaic, Christian, and Islamic) view of time is that history proceeds in a rigidly linear way, with a definite beginning and end point. Sanatana Dharma, on the other hand, understands that time is cyclical in the same way that all of nature is cyclical. Thus, we proceed through a succession of four grand ages (*yugas*), in the same way that nature precedes through the seasons. Each of these *yugas*, in turn, contains mini-cycles within them. Currently, we are in the fourth of these ages, known as the Kali Yuga, or the Age of Conflict.

"Kali-yuga is the ocean of all sins and sorrows, but it has one great merit, that those who do *kirtana* or meditate upon the holy names of Sri Krishna attain the highest love, peace and freedom from material bondage. The people of this age get the same benefit by *kirtana* or meditating upon the holy names, as they did by meditation on Lord Vishnu in Satya-yuga, by sacrifices in Treta-yuga and by worship in Dvapara-yuga." (*Srimad Bhagavatam*, 12.3.51-52)

9. Historical Devolution

Connected to the concept of the cyclicality of ages is the understanding that each successive age becomes less Dharmic and more unspiritual than the preceding one. Thus, humanity devolves in its spiritual and ethical behavior, as well as in its aesthetic appreciation and development. The notion that human society is progressing is a very recent idea that is no more than three hundred years old. The entire ancient world was in agreement that the opposite is the case. Human society devolves over time.

"[In the Kali Yuga] the whole world will be filled with subhuman behavior and notions, and ceremonies and sacrifices will cease, and joy will be nowhere, and general rejoicing will disappear. And men will rob the possessions of helpless persons, of those that are friendless, and of wise people also. And, possessed of small energy and strength, without knowledge and given to avarice and folly and malevolent practices, men will accept with joy the gifts made by wicked people with words of contempt. And, O son of Kunti, the kings of the earth, with hearts wedded to evil without knowledge and always boastful of their wisdom, will challenge one another from desire of taking one another's life." (*Mahabharata, Vanaparva*, 189)

10. Transcendent Authority

Authority and knowledge are deductive, not inductive. They are derived from sources that are transcendental and qualitatively higher, and never from lower sources. Truth comes from above, not below. Truth is not arrived at by democratic vote, or by the demands of the masses, but by learning from those sources that are closest to the original Source. Such sources include God, the *guru*, Shastra (the Vedic scriptures), the wise people of the past, and such higher benevolent beings as the *devas* and *devis* (gods and goddesses). Authority and truth always come from above, and never from below.

11. Order of Philosopher Guides

Every civilized society was at one time guided by an organized sacred order of spiritual teachers and philosophers. In ancient Celtic society, for example, this sacred order was known as the Druids. They were similarly known as the Gothar in Nordic society. In the most ancient strata of Vedic society, this order of guides is known as the *Brahmanas*, or "those who know Brahman (God)". In our current age, which is the sixth millennium of the Kali Yuga (or the 21st century of the common era), the atheistic leaders who presently control our planet have purposefully destroyed all of the traditional orders of spiritual guides. The International Sanatana Dharma Society is currently in the process of reestablishing an order of pure *brahmanas* to help guide us toward a Vedic restoration.

"O Lord, You are the supreme director of the brahminical culture. Your considering the *brahmanas* to be in the highest position is Your example for teaching others. Actually You are the supreme worshipable Deity, not only for the gods but for the *brahmanas* also." (*Srimad Bhagavatam*, 3.16.17)

"Whoever acquires the brahminical qualifications - whose only treasure is good behavior - who is grateful and who takes shelter of experienced persons gets all the opulence of the world. I therefore wish that the Supreme Godhead and His associates be pleased with the *brahmana* class, with the cows and with me." (*Srimad Bhagavatam*, 4.21.44)

"The *Vedas* are My eternal transcendental sound incarnation. Therefore the *Vedas* are *shabda-brahma* (the Word of God). In this world, the *brahmanas* thoroughly study all the *Vedas*, and because they assimilate the Vedic conclusions, they are also to be considered the *Vedas* personified. The *brahmanas* are situated in the supreme transcendental mode of nature - *sattva-guna*. Because of this, they are fixed in control of their minds, sense control, and truthfulness. They describe the *Vedas* in their original sense, and out of mercy they teach the purpose of the *Vedas* to all conditioned souls. They practice austerity and tolerance, and they realize the position of the living entity and the Supreme Lord. These are the eight qualifications of the *brahmanas*. Therefore among all living entities, no one is superior to the *brahmanas*." (*Srimad Bhagavatam*, 5.5.24)

12. Philosopher-King

The Chakravartin, or Philosopher-King, is considered to be the most perfect form of spiritual-political leader. Such a leader personifies in his being the very best simultaneous qualities of the sage and the warrior, the saint and the administrator, the priest and the king. The Chakravartin is the most rare of leaders, and descends upon the Earth with the purpose of establishing a Dharma civilization. When a Chakravartin rules a nation, that nation becomes a Heaven on Earth.

"The king who is well educated and disciplined in sciences, devoted to good Government of his subjects, and bent on doing good to all people will enjoy the earth unopposed." (*Kautilya Artha Shastra*, book 1, chapter 5)

"A king and a *brahmana* deeply versed in the *Vedas*, these two uphold the moral order in the world." (*Gautama Dharma Sutras*, 8:1)

"The proper function of the head of state is to govern according to Dharma and not merely to enjoy the luxuries of life." (Mahabharata, *Shantiparva*, 90.3)

13. **Theomorphism**

This is the principle that states that everything that exists has God as both its origin and archetypal model. Everything in existence has God as its origin, either directly or indirectly. As such, all living beings share in God's positive attributes. God is free, thus we are free. God exists eternally, thus we exist eternally. God is good, therefore we are good in our innermost spiritual essence. God is not made in man's image. We are made in God's image.

> *Aham sarvasya prabhavo mattah sarvam pravartate*
> *iti matva bhajante mam budha bhava-samanvitah*

"I am the source of all spiritual and material realities. Everything emanates from Me. The wise who know this truth perfectly engage in devotional service toward Me, and worship Me with all their being." (*Bhagavad Gita*, 10:8)

14. **Conservation of Energy**

All material energy (*prakriti*) is constant and is conserved over time. It is never created or destroyed, but is merely reformulated into different names and forms (*nama* and *rupa*) in accordance with the physical laws of Dharma. The material energy (Shakti) ultimately has its source and predominant organizing principle in the supreme energetic (Shaktiman), who is God.

> Question: How have you personally witnessed some or all of these 14 principles of Dharma in operation either in your own life or in the world around you?

> Exercise: Always be aware of, and operate within, these principles of Dharma in your daily life.

2.1.10 The Divine Descent of Dharma

God relates to us through grace and love. That grace and love become transformed into Dharma when it descends into the material world in order to serve as a divine mechanism through which we can access that grace and again transcend materiality. What we call "Dharma" in the context of its operational presence in the material world is actually the same as what we would term God's grace in the spiritual world. Dharma is a manifestation of the grace of God.

Everything in existence is ultimately upheld by the grace of God. That grace becomes transformed (and so more accessible) in accordance to the level of being that one is in.

> 1) That grace is known in its full form when we are in the liberated state, and thus able to experience that grace purely and directly.
> 2) It becomes a bit denser in the form of Dharma, which is the same grace, but transformed into the form of the natural metaphysical laws of the universe.

3) Finally, that same grace becomes transformed into the very laws of physics itself and serves as the physical operating principles of our cosmos.

So, the laws of physics - without which even material reality would not function - are really the grace of God as well, but just applied to physicality. Without physical laws, we would not be able to even exist in the material world. Thus, we are always surrounded by grace, but we have different relationships with it, and perceive it differently, in accordance with the state of being that we are speaking of.

"He created still further the most excellent Dharma. Dharma is the ruling power of all ruling powers, therefore there is nothing higher than Dharma. Thenceforth even a less powerful man rules a stronger with the help of Dharma, as with the help of a king." (*Brihadaranyaka Upanishad*, 1.4.14)

> *ananyash chintayanto mam ye janah paryupasate*
> *tesham nityabhiyuktanam yoga-kshemam vahamy aham*

"But those who worship Me with devotion, meditating on My transcendental form--to them I carry what they lack and preserve what they have." (*Bhagavad Gita*, 9.22)

> Questions: How have you experienced the grace of God in your own life? How does God's grace uphold reality and benefit humanity?

2.1.11 The Behavioral Principles of Dharma

There are several principles of behavior that are found in Sanatana Dharma that become reflected onto the person who upholds Dharma is his own life. Some of these include cleanliness, honesty, loyalty, seeking excellence, etc. The list of such positive virtues is indeed long. Such principles are seen in the day-to-day behavior of the Dharmi and constitute a healthy Dharma lifestyle. In this specific section of the book *Sanatana Dharma: The Eternal Natural Way*, we outline a few of these behavioral principles. We have also included these in the section below.

"Non-violence, truthfulness, not acquiring illegitimate wealth, purity and control of senses are, in brief, the Dharma (Natural Law) for all people, regardless of their individual psychophysical natures (*varnas*)." (*Manava Dharma Shastra*, 10.63)

"Truthfulness, to be free from anger, sharing wealth with others, forgiveness, procreation of children from one's wife alone, purity, absence of enmity, straightforwardness and maintaining persons dependent on oneself are the nine rules of the Dharma of all persons regardless of their individual psychophysical natures (*varnas*)." (*Mahabharata, Shantiparva*, 6.8)

A small sample of the positive behavior that the Dharmi tries to follow include the following:

1. Reverence for nature, an attraction to spending time in nature, and deep environmentalism.

2. God-centeredness. Endeavoring to experience God's presence at all times.

3. Exhibiting nobility in all of one's thoughts, words, and deeds.

4. Observing an organic lifestyle that is close to the Earth (Bhudevi).

5. Cultivating a regular and deep meditation practice.

6. Veneration and reverence for our own biological ancestors.

7. Acquiring wisdom (*vidya*), philosophical discernment, as well as intellectual and aesthetic discrimination.

8. Having a life of healthy wellbeing - physical, mental, and spiritual.

9. Avid cleanliness in body, mind, and surroundings.

10. Seeking excellence in all endeavors.

11. Humility.

12. Fearlessness.

13. Self-discipline.

14. Cultivating strong and healthy family units.

15. Admiration of beauty.

16. Honesty.

17. Loyalty.

18. Truthfulness.

Question: Which of these virtues do I especially need to work on cultivating?

Exercise: Choose one of these virtues and avidly work on increasing it within yourself for an entire week. Then choose another virtue to work on the next week, and so on.

2.2.1 The Epistemological Principles of Dharma

All philosophy begins with what is called epistemology, that is, the question of what are the mechanisms through which a person can know truth. In other words, before we can even begin to answer the question "What is truth?" first we must be able to answer the even more basic question of "How can we know truth?" What is the proper source for accessing knowledge of transcendental realities? In the rest of this section of chapter two, and continuing into chapter three, we tackle this important issue from the Vedic perspective.

"The *Veda* is the first source of Dharma. The exposition by the Seers (*rishis*), handed down from generation to generation by memory, the virtuous conduct of those who are well-versed in the *Veda*, and lastly, what is agreeable to the good conscience, are the other sources of Dharma." (*Manava Dharma Shastra*, 2.6)

"The Supreme Lord cannot be obtained by one who is qualified by being a great lecturer, a great scholar, or a great student of the Vedic literature. The Lord reveals His own form to one with whom He is pleased." (*Katha Upanishad*, 1.2.23)

Contemplation: Our eyes are not powerful enough to see through a wall and into the next room. Yet the atheists demand "show me God!" Our minds are not large enough to contain even 1% of the world's accumulated knowledge. Yet the atheists claim to have the knowledge to declare that there is no God. The analytic power of our intellects has now been surpassed by laptops, tablet computers and smart phones. Yet the atheists claim we can disprove the Transcendent via logic alone. Atheism is predicated upon arrogance, not reason.

2.2.2 Three Necessary Factors of Knowing

There are three elements that have to be present for us to be able to know anything. These three elements are:

(a) The knower. The person who seeks to know (*pramatr*).

(b) The object that the person seeks to know (*prameya*).

(c) The proper medium (*pramana*), or means, through which the seeker obtains the object of knowledge.

If you want to know if your keys are on the table, you look at the table. In this example, you are the knower (the person who wants the knowledge), the object of knowledge is the set of keys (the thing to be known), the proper medium of knowledge that you use to find the keys/object are your eyes (the tool, or medium, of knowing).

"Perception is that knowledge which arises from the contact of a sense with its object and which is determinate, unnamable and non-erratic." (*Nyaya Sutras*, 4)

> Question: What is the proper medium of knowledge that you would use if the object you wish to know is a mathematical equation? For example: 1+1 =? What is the proper medium to use if you want to know God?

2.2.3 Three Ways of Knowing

In addition the three factors of knowing, there are three distinct tools that we can use to know three different, corresponding types of objects of knowledge. These are:

> 1) Empiricism (*pratyaksha*), or knowing material objects through the senses.
>
> 2) Reasoning and inference (*anumana*), or knowing intellectual objects, such as math and logic, through the intellect.

3) Spiritual experience and scriptures (*shabda*), or knowing the nature of consciousness, including our own souls and God, through yogic means.

We can only know material objects through the senses. We can only know the answers to mathematical and logical problems through the intellect. It is only through the third tool, *shabda*, that we can know transcendental Truth.

pratyakshas-cha anumanan cha shastran cha vividhagamam
trayam suviditam karyam dharma-shuddhim-abhishata

"If one wants to understand what is reality, one must consider the three kinds of evidence: Vedic evidence, perception, and inference."
(*Manava Dharma Shastra*, 12.105)

Question: Why is it that we cannot know God as an object of knowledge by using the tools of either sense perception (*pratyaksha*) or reason (*anumana*)?

Exercise: Try to answer the mathematical problem 597 x 674 without using your intellect (even if you are using a calculator, you must use your mind and intellect to enter the numbers!). Try counting the leaves of a small tree without using your senses.

2.2.4 Truth Verification System

None of the propositions presented by Sanatana Dharma are to be merely accepted through blind faith. Sanatana Dharma has never been based upon blind faith. Indeed, this is one of the biggest differences between Sanatana Dharma and the Abrahamic traditions (Judaism, Christianity and Islam). Rather, followers of Dharma use a three-limbed verification system to ascertain whether any doctrine, teaching or claim is actually true. These three tools of verification are:

1) Shastra: The revealed Vedic scriptures.
2) Acharya: The guidance of self-realized sages.
3) Vichara: Our own reasoning capacity and experience.

When you are in any doubt as to whether or not a teaching is actually authentically reflecting the eternal truth, test that teaching against this threefold verification system. If the teachings are refuted by any one of these three, then it is not true.

"The root of Dharma is the entire *Veda*; the traditions and practices of those who know the *Veda*; the conduct of good people; and what is acceptable to oneself." (*Manava Dharma Shastra*, 2.6)

"Logic and arguments are insufficient to understand the Absolute Truth." (*Brahma Sutras*, 2.1.11)

Questions: If a *guru* tells you that following the Vedic scriptures (Shastra) is of no importance in spiritual life, which is clearly contradicted in the scriptures themselves (see *Manava Dharma Shastra*, 2.6, above), would he or she be telling you the truth? Is that person really an authentic *guru*? Should you continue to follow a false guru who has demonstrated that what he is teaching is contrary to the scriptures?

Chapter 3 Epistemology in Literary Form: The Scriptures of Sanatana Dharma

In this chapter, we look at the vast array of books that constitute the Vedic literature, which are the perfect, non-manmade and eternal truth in literary form.

"We offer our obeisances again and again to You, who are the basis of all authoritative evidence, who are the author and ultimate source of the revealed scriptures, and who have manifested Yourself in those Vedic literatures that explain the course of practical activities in this world, as well as in those that explain the nature of Transcendent Reality." (*Srimad Bhagavatam*, 10.16.44)

3.1.1 The Vedic Literature

The *rishis* were ordinary human beings who, through the intense practice of Yoga and meditation discipline, became liberated beings. These ancient *rishis* (perfected seer-sages) were the revealers of the divine knowledge contained in the *Vedas*. For the follower of Sanatana Dharma, all spiritual authority is derived from the Vedic literature. We look to the Vedic scriptures for guidance in all spiritual, philosophical, ethical and yogic practice matters. The stories of the sages, pious kings and righteous gods that are found in the scriptures provide us with models of behavior for daily living. Indeed, we have so much assurance in the loving guidance of the Vedic scriptures that it is understood that we are to reject any spiritual practice or philosophical proposition that cannot be supported by our scriptures. The Vedic scriptures are the personification of Truth that we can access in the form of literature.

"The power of inference is limited to producing conclusions regarding the general. It does not have the power to determine the particular. Therefore one should seek out the particulars concerning God, such as His name(s), from the authoritative scriptural tradition." (*Vyasa-bhashya, Yoga Sutras*, 1.25)

> Questions: What was the first Vedic scripture that you ever read? What impact did it have on you?

3.1.2 Genres of the Vedic Scriptural Canon

There are many genres of literature among the Vedic scriptures. All of these genres fall under the two main headings of *Shruti* and *Smriti*. *Shruti* consists of those works that are heard directly from the *rishis* (Vedic Seers), and *Smriti* are those sacred texts that were written down several generations after being revealed by the *rishis*. Both categories, however, are considered to be Vedic and are thus sacred.

Followers of Sanatana Dharma accept only the Vedic revelation as legitimate scriptures. We do not accept Abrahamic books, such as the Old Testament, all the writings of Paul in the New Testament, or the Qur'an as having any authoritative validity. We do not seek guidance in these Abrahamic scriptures.

There are several sacred texts that are not overtly Vedic, however, that we do accept as acceptable guides on our path to knowing Truth. We do, for example, view the direct words of Jesus contained in the Gospels,[5] as well as the Tao Te Ching, and some of the earliest sermons of the Buddha as having significant spiritual authority. Ultimately, however, it is always the Vedic scriptures themselves that serve as our highest spiritual authority and guide.

"A person who is constantly engaged in reading literature enunciating the cultivation of Vaishnava devotional service is always glorious in human society, and certainly Lord Krishna becomes pleased with him. A person who very carefully keeps such literature at home and offers respectful obeisances to it becomes freed from all sinful reactions and ultimately becomes worshipable by the demigods (*devas*)." (*Skanda Purana*)

---

[5] We would include several of the Gnostic Gospels and texts among the list of acceptable non-Vedic texts.

Question: What is the unique process by which the *rishis* revealed the Vedic scriptures?

Exercise: After you have finished your daily meditation, perform the following practice. Read a verse from one of the Vedic scriptures, for example from the *Bhagavad Gita*, the *Upanishads*, or the *Narada Bhakti Sutras*, and spend several minutes contemplating the meaning of the verse with a peaceful and serene mind. Allow the verse to truly speak to your mind and heart.

The following diagram illustrates many of the most important Vedic scriptures.

The Vedic Canon

Shruti	**Smriti**
Samhitas (Vedas)	*Puranas*
Brahmanas	*Sutras*
Aranyakas	*Pancharatras*
Upanishads	*Agamas*
	Tantras
	Dharma Shastras[6]
	Vedangas
	Upavedas
	Itihasas (Two Epics)
	1. *Ramayana*
	2. *Mahabharata*
	2(a) *Bhagavad Gita*

---

[6] The *Yajnavalkya Smrti* (1.4-5) lists 24 *Dharma Shastras: Manu, Atri, Vishnu, Harita, Yajnavalkya, Ushana, Angira, Yama, Apastamba, Samvarta, Katyayana, Brhaspati, Parashara, Vyasa, Sankha, Likhita, Daksha, Gautama, Shatatapa, Vashishtha.*

40

3.2.1 Important Scriptures

While all of the Vedic scriptures are of importance, there are several principal works that stand out due to their more accessible and philosophical nature. These include:

a) The four *Veda-Samhitas*

b) The major *Upanishads*

c) The *Puranas*

d) The *Sutras*

e) The *Bhagavad Gita*

Of all the Vedic scriptures, however, the most important for us to read and study today include.

1) *Bhagavad Gita*

2) *Srimad Bhagavatam* (also known as the *Bhagavata Purana*)

3) The 12 major *Upanishads*[7]

4) *Narada Bhakti Sutras*

5) *Yoga Sutras*

Starting in 2015, the International Sanatana Dharma Society will begin offering translations and commentaries on all these important scriptures.

---

[7] The twelve major *Upanishads* are: *Isha Upanishad, Kena Upanishad, Katha Upanishad, Prashna Upanishad, Mundaka Upanishad, Mandukya Upanishad, Taittiriya Upanishad, Aitareya Upanishad, Chandogya Upanishad, Brihadaranyaka Upanishad, Shvetashvatara Upanishad, Narayana Upanishad.*

"Sri Vishnu said, 'I Myself have manifested in the form of the *Bhagavad Gita*. Please understand that the first five chapters are My five heads, the next ten chapters are My ten arms, and the sixteenth chapter is My stomach. The last two chapters are My lotus-feet. In this way you should understand the transcendental Deity of the *Bhagavad Gita*. This *Bhagavad Gita* is the destroyer of all evils. And that intelligent person who daily recites one chapter or even one verse, one half verse, or at least one quarter verse, will attain the same position as a liberated person (*susharma*) has attained.'" (*Gita Mahatmya*, chapter 1)

> Fact: The sacred nature of these Vedic scriptures is recognized to be so powerful that even having them in one's home makes the environment more auspicious and peaceful. If you can, try to have copies in your home of a) the *Bhagavad Gita*, b) the *Srimad Bhagavatam*, c) the 12 major *Upanishads*, d) the *Narada Bhakti Sutras*, and e) the *Yoga Sutras*.

3.2.2 The Four Veda Samhitas

The four *Veda Samhitas* are primarily a collection of hymns addressed to the *devas* and *devis* (gods and goddesses). Though there is not as much of philosophical content in these four works as in many of the other scriptures, these four mantric works are of great importance for the positive, elevating effect that they have on the listener when they are chanted. It produces a very powerful meditative experience on the listener to meditate on the sound of the *Veda Samhitas* being recited.

"Even though situated in a material body, one who is fully aware of the path of the ancestors and the path of the gods that is recommended in the *Vedas*, and who thus opens his eyes through the study of the *Vedas*, is never bewildered." (*Srimad Bhagavatam*, 7.15.56)

42

Question: What are the names of the four *Veda Samhitas*?

3.2.3 Upanishads

The *Upanishads* are highly philosophical works that form the basis of Vedanta (the culmination of the *Vedas*) philosophy. *'Upa'-'ni'-'shad'* means "sitting close to" because these works consist of many conversations in which the disciple is sitting at the feet of the *guru* and receiving sacred instructions from the *guru*. There are 108 major *Upanishads*,[8] of which the following twelve are considered the most important.

1. *Isha Upanishad*
2. *Kena Upanishad*
3. *Katha Upanishad*
4. *Prashna Upanishad*
5. *Mundaka Upanishad*
6. *Mandukya Upanishad*
7. *Taittiriya Upanishad*
8. *Aitareya Upanishad*
9. *Chandogya Upanishad*
10. *Brihadaranyaka Upanishad*
11. *Shvetashvatara Upanishad*
12. *Narayana Upanishad*

"The disciple said; 'Teach me, sir, the *Upanishad.*' The preceptor replied: 'I have already told you the *Upanishad.* I have certainly told you the *Upanishad* is about Brahman.'" (*Kena Upanishad*, 4.7)

"Take the *Upanishad* as the bow, the great weapon, and place upon it the arrow sharpened by meditation. Then, having drawn it back with a mind directed to the thought of Brahman, strike that mark, O my good friend -

---

[8] Of a total of 220 *Upanishads* that we still have today.

that which is the Imperishable." (*Mundaka Upanishad*, 2.2.3)

> Guidance: The *Upanishads* are very densely philosophical books
> that are difficult to understand without the expert guidance of a
> guru or a good teacher. The easiest of the *Upanishads* to start
> with are probably the *Isha Upanishad*, the *Katha Upanishad*, and
> the *Narayana Upanishad*.

3.2.4 Puranas

The *Puranas* are some of the most beautifully presented of the Vedic
scriptures, since they are a combination of sacred stories, histories of the
world and the universe, and engaging philosophical dialogues. The two
most important of these large books are the *Vishnu Purana* and the *Bhagavata Purana*, which is also known as the *Srimad Bhagavatam*.

itihasa-puranah panchamah vedanam vedah

"The *Itihasa* and *Puranas* are the 5th *Veda*." (*Chandogya Upanishad*, 7.1.4)

"Just as the Mother Ganga is the greatest of all rivers, Lord Achyuta Hari
the greatest among worshiped deities, and Lord Shambhu Shiva the
greatest of Vaishnavas, so *Srimad Bhagavatam* is the greatest of all *Puranas*." (*Srimad Bhagavatam*, 12.13.16)

> Guidance: The very best translation of the *Srimad Bhagavatam* is
> the multi-volume edition, with extensive commentary, done by
> A.C. Bhaktivedanta Swami Prabhupada. In a few years, I will al-
> so be providing a translation and commentary on several
> hundred of the most important verses of the *Srimad Bhagavatam*.

3.2.5 Sutra Literature

The *Sutra* works are very unique in that they are meant to communicate the essence of a specific philosophical school in a very brief, code-like construction known as *sutras*, or "threads". Every important Vedic philosophical school has at least one *Sutra* text that describes its teachings. Thus, there is a *Sutra* book for the Yoga school, the Vedanta school, as well as for Mimamsa, Nyaya, Vaisheshika, Samkhya, Bhakti, etc. Due to their purposeful brevity, it is very difficult to fully comprehend the very deep teachings that these books are trying to convey without the benefit of a very qualified *guru*, which is exactly the intent of this form of writing. Some of the more famous of these numerous *Sutras* include: *Brahma Sutras*, *Narada Bhakti Sutras* and *Yoga Sutras* of Patanjali.

"Now, then, is the time to inquire into the nature of the Absolute." (*Brahma Sutras*, 1.1.1)

'Now, therefore, we shall expound upon devotional consciousness." (*Narada Bhakti Sutras*, 1.1)

"Now commences the study of Yoga." (*Yoga Sutras*, 1.1)

"Now, then, is the time to inquire into the nature of devotional consciousness." (*Shandilya Bhakti Sutras*, 1.1)

> Questions: Many of the *Sutras* begin by stating that "Now is the time to begin studying **x**". Why do they begin in this way? What is it assumed that the reader was doing previous to reading the *Sutra*?

3.3.1 The Bhagavad Gita

Of all the many books in the library of Vedic literature, the most important for us today is the *Bhagavad Gita*. This is the case for several reasons: a) the *Bhagavad Gita* presents the reader with the most perfectly constructed and systematic essential teachings of the totality of all the Vedic scriptures; b) having taught the *Bhagavad Gita* just as the last *yuga* (age) was ending, and the present one beginning, it is an instruction that was especially designed for the residents of our age; c) it was spoken not just by a great sage or *yogi*, but directly by the *avatara* (incarnation) of God, Sri Krishna. The *Bhagavad Gita* is the scripture of our age, and Sri Krishna is the form of God who is to be especially worshiped for our age.

"Though engaged in the performance of worldly duties, one who is regular in the study of the *Bhagavad Gita* becomes free. He is a happy person in this world. He is not bound by *karma*." (*Gita Mahatmya*, 2)

> Questions: When did you first read the *Bhagavad Gita*? What impact did that reading have on you? Do you still read it on a regular basis?

3.3.2 Central Importance of the Bhagavad Gita

The importance of the *Bhagavad Gita* has been recognized by the greatest spiritual authorities all throughout of history, including by many of the leading intellectuals of the Western world. The teachings of the *Bhagavad Gita* are designed to help liberate the entire world, and not merely a small geographical part of it. It is the scripture of our age.

"One may cleanse himself daily by taking a bath in water, but if one takes a bath even once in the sacred Ganges water of the *Bhagavad Gita*, for him the dirt of material life is altogether vanquished." (*Gita Mahatmya*, 3)

> Fact: The *Bhagavad Gita* is translated into almost every language in the world today. There are about 700 translations of the *Bhagavad Gita* in English alone!

3.3.3 The Outer and Inner Wars

The story of the *Bhagavad Gita* involves two wars. The first was an actual historical war that took place almost 5200 years ago, known as the Mahabharata War. This great world war ushered in our present era, known as the Kali Yuga. The other war that the *Bhagavad Gita* is speaking of is a metaphorical inner war that takes place within us all in the form of our own individual spiritual struggle to transcend illusion and to achieve full liberation (*moksha*).

> "Considering your specific duty as a Dharma warrior, you should know that there is no better engagement for you than fighting for Dharma; and so there is no need for hesitation." (*Bhagavad Gita*, 2.31)

> Questions: In what ways has your own struggle toward spiritual emancipation been similar to a war? What injuries and scars have you experienced in your life? What is your strategy for victory?

3.3.4 Earth's First World War

This section of the book presents a brief and straightforward retelling of the story of the Mahabharata War, the outer war of the *Bhagavad Gita*.

"Never was there a time when I did not exist, nor you, nor all these kings; nor in the future shall any of us cease to be." (*Bhagavad Gita*, 2.12)

3.3.5 The Inner War

It is specifically in that portion of the story in which the great warrior Arjuna begins to lose hope and succumb to depression that the inner war portion of the *Bhagavad Gita* begins. It is at this point that Arjuna, in his despair, wisely turns to Bhagavan Sri Krishna as his friend and *guru*, and seeks His divine counsel at this time of greatest need. In his proceeding actions and questions to Lord Krishna, Arjuna is representing not only himself, but is representative of us all in our turning toward God in philosophical inquiry and at times of trouble.

> *karpanya-dosopahata-svabhavah*
> *prcchami tvam dharma sammudha-chetah*
> *yac chreyah syan niscitam bruhi tan me*
> *shishyas te'ham sadhi mam tvam prapannam*

"Now I am confused about my duty and have lost all composure because of weakness. In this condition I am asking you to tell me clearly what is best for me. Now I am your disciple, and a soul surrendered unto You. Please instruct me." (*Bhagavad Gita*, 2:7)

> Questions: Have you experienced bouts of depression, fear and hopelessness in your own life? Who did you turn to for trusted advice and guidance?

> Guidance: Arjuna was blessed over 5100 years ago to be able to turn directly to God, who was there standing before him, as his personal *guru*. Today, we are to turn to a presently living and qualified person who can serve as our *guru*.

3.3.6 The Philosophical Divisions of the Bhagavad Gita

The great sage Yamuna Acharya (10th century CE) explained that the 18 chapters of the *Bhagavad Gita* could be divided into several philosophical sections.

> Chapters 1-6 focus on *atma-jnana*, or self-realization.
>
> Chapters 7-12 focus on Bhakti Yoga, or the means by which we revive our natural devotional consciousness.
>
> Chapters 13-18 focus on deeper philosophical clarification of the teachings of the previous 12 chapters.

"He who recites the eighteen chapters of the *Bhagavad Gita* daily, with a pure and unshaken mind, attains perfection in knowledge, and reaches the highest state or supreme goal." (*Gita Mahatmya*, 10)

> Questions: What are you truly seeking in your spiritual pursuit? Are you seeking self-realization, God-consciousness, or both? Are you seeking something more ego or materially oriented?
>
> Questions II: What philosophical questions are you seeking the answers to? Where in the *Bhagavad Gita* are these questions addressed?

3.3.7 The Unity of Yoga

In this important section, we show that the four *yogas* that are presented in the *Bhagavad Gita* are designed to be practiced as one Yoga system, with *bhakti* (devotional consciousness) as the very heart of all Yoga practice. Thus, the *Bhagavad Gita* presents a unified and integrated Yoga system, and not multiple Yogas.

bhaktya mam abhijanati yavan yas chasmi tattvatah
tato mam tattvato jnatva visate tad-anantaram

"One can understand Me as I am only by devotional contemplation. And when one is in full consciousness of Me by such devotion, he can enter into My truth." (*Bhagavad Gita*, 18:55)

bhaktya tv ananyaya sakya aham evam-vidho'rjuna
jnatum drashtum cha tattvena praveshtum cha parantapa

"...only by devotional meditation can I be understood as I am, standing before you, and can thus be seen directly. In this way you can enter into the mysteries of My being" (*Bhagavad Gita*, 11:54)

manmana bhava mad-bhakto mad-yaji mam namaskuru
mam evaishyasi satyam te pratijane priyo'si me

"Always think of Me and become My devotee," declares Krishna, "worship Me and offer your homage unto Me. Thus you will come to Me without fail. I promise you this because you are My very dear friend." (*Bhagavad Gita*, 18:65)

sarva-dharman parityajya mam ekam sharanam vraja
aham tvam sarva-papebhyo mokshayishyami ma shucah

"Abandon all varieties of lesser *dharmas* [duties, lesser paths] and simply surrender unto Me. I shall deliver you from all demeritorious reactions. Do not fear." (*Bhagavad Gita*, 18:66)

Chapter 4 Metaphysics: The Nature of Reality

Chapter four deals with Sanatana Dharma's views on metaphysics, or those topics that lay outside of the physical domain. Philosophically, chapters four and five are two of the most important chapters of the book *Sanatana Dharma: The Eternal Natural Way*.

4.1.1 Tri-Tattva: The Metaphysical Foundations of Reality

All of chapters four and five will deal with what are called the Tri-Tattva, or the Three Reals, from a variety of perspectives. These three elements of reality together constitute the very foundation of all reality, and thus the foundation of Sanatana Dharma metaphysics. If a person has a good grasp of the nature of the Tri-Tattvas, then he has understood the basis of Vedanta.

"Although I am one, I shall become many." (*Chandogya Upanishad*, 6.2.3)

4.1.2 The Three Reals

The Three Reals are:

A) Atman, or individual units of consciousness (souls).

B) Brahman, or God.

C) Jagat, or insentient materiality.

Everything in existence that is either perceivable or conceivable falls into one, and only one, of these three categories.

"Two birds, inseparable friends, cling to the same tree. One of them eats the sweet fruit of the tree, but the other looks on without eating." (*Mundaka Upanishad*, 3.1.1)[9]

> Questions: Observe everything currently around you that you can either detect with your senses or else think about. Into which category of the Three Reals does each individual item belong? Where do the walls of your home belong; your soul; God?

4.1.3 Atman – The True Self

Atman is one of the Three Reals of Sanatana Dharma. *Atman* means an individual unit of consciousness. Each of us is ultimately *atman*, which is our true self. Our individual *atman* has Brahman (God, or Paramatman, the Supreme Atman) as its source. As a result, the Atman is a finite and dependent reflection of Brahman. Since Brahman is our source, just like Brahman we are eternal (*sanatana*) and incorruptible (*adushya*). We are cognizant knowers (*chit*) and full of bliss (*ananda*). The goal of self-realization (*atma-jnana*) is to know our Atman, our own true self.

"Know the *atman* as the passenger of the chariot, the body as the chariot itself, the intellect as the charioteer, and the mind as the reins. The senses are said to be the horses and selfish desires are the roads they travel. When the *atman* is confused with the body, mind and senses, they say that he appears to enjoy pleasures and suffer sorrows." (*Katha Upanishad*, 1.3.3–4)

---

[9] In this famous story from the *Mundaka Upanishad*, the first bird, who is selfishly eating the fruit of the tree, represents Atman. The second bird, who serves as a detached witness and friend of the first bird, is Brahman. The tree itself is Jagat, the field of illusory enjoyment.

"Never was there a time when I did not exist, nor you, nor all these kings; nor in the future shall any of us cease to be." (*Bhagavad Gita*, 2.12)

"As the embodied soul continuously passes, in this body, from boyhood to youth to old age, the soul similarly passes into another body at death. A sober person is not bewildered by such a change." (*Bhagavad Gita*, 2.13)

> Guidance: The search for self-realization is the first step in the journey toward liberation. Before we can know anything else, we must first know the knower.

4.1.4 Brahman – The Absolute

Brahman is another of the Three Reals of Sanatana Dharma. Brahman is the philosophical description of God as being that from which all things proceed. Brahman is one, perfect, good and is the source of an infinite number of auspicious attributes, all of which are full and unsurpassable to an infinite degree.

janmady asya yataha

"Brahman is that from which all things proceed." (*Brahma Sutras*, 1.1.2)

"He is the God of infinite forms, in whose glory all things are, smaller than the smallest atom, and yet the creator of all, ever living in the mystery of His creation. In the vision of this God of love there is everlasting peace." (*Shvetashvatara Upanishad*, 4.14)

> Guidance: In our continuing journey on the path to full spiritual liberation, the highest attainment that we can achieve is God-consciousness (*Brahma-vidya*). This stage comes after self-

realization.

Questions: In our spiritual search, are we seeking the tenth highest, the third highest, the second highest, or truly the very highest reality? If we are truly seeking the highest, then we must not be satisfied with anything less than full God-realization.

4.1.5 Jagat – The Power of Prime Materiality Enformed

Jagat is the third of the Three Reals of Sanatana Dharma. It is also known as Prakriti. When we examine anything around us, we are detecting objects that have one of three natures. These things are either a) sentient (of the nature of consciousness), b) insentient (of the nature of materiality), or c) sentience temporarily situated within insentience (as in an *atman* inhabiting a physical body due to having fallen into illusion). Jagat designates the second of these, insentient materiality itself. Anything that is purely material is Jagat.

"The Manifest (Jagat) is composed of the three attributes (*gunas*), is non-discriminated, objective, general, non-intelligent and productive. So also is Nature. The Purusha (Atman) is the reverse of that, as well as similar." (*Samkhya Karika*, 11)

Question: Is your body Atman, Brahman or Jagat?

Fact: The emotions, mind, intellect and false ego are all considered to be aspects of Jagat, or materiality.

4.1.6 Inter-relationships Between the Tri-Tattvas

Most *atmans* (individual souls) who are currently residing in the material world, suffering from a self-imposed illusory state, mistakenly see themselves as being in an adversarial relationship with the other elements of reality. They unconsciously see Brahman and Jagat, as well as even with other *atmans*, as their supposed enemies. Thus, most living beings are experiencing an imbalance in the inter-relationship between Atman, Brahman and Jagat. We can interpret the goal of liberation as including a restoration of balance between these three elements. The Tri-Tattvas are meant to be working in perfect harmony with one another, and not being at odds in the illusioned minds of individual beings.

"Earth, water, fire, air, ether, mind, intelligence and false ego - all together these eight constitute My separated material energies." (*Bhagavad Gita*, 7.4)

"This is the nature of the divinity of the Supreme Godhead: He is not affected by the qualities of material nature, even though He is in contact with them. Similarly, the devotees who have taken shelter of the Supreme do not become influenced by the material qualities." (*Srimad Bhagavatam*, 1.11.38)

Questions: Under which of the Three Reals does mind fall? What about intelligence?

Contemplation: As you sit and contemplate all the different components that make up who you are as a person, where do the individual Tattvas fit in? What parts of you are purely material? What part of you is the *atman*? Where is God?

4.2.1 Tri-tattva and the Three Dharmic Paths

There are three distinct paths (*margas*) discernible in the Vedic tradition:

a) Vaishnava, b) Shaiva, and c) Shakta.

These paths all have three different goals, and are motivated by different desires in the person who decides to follow one path over the other two. These three paths correspond with each of the Tri-Tattvas and with three distinct deities.

The Vaishnava path is concerned with Brahman and worships Narayana. The Shaiva path is concerned with Atman and worships Shiva as the personification of Atman. The Shakta path is concerned with Jagat (or *prakriti*) and worships Shakti Devi. It is, thus, only by following the Vaishnava path of devotion to Narayana that once can directly know God most truly and fully.

Tattva	Marga	Deity	Sadhana	Scripture
Brahman	Vaishnava	Narayana	Ashtanga	Prasthana Traya[10]
Atman	Shaiva	Shiva	Hatha	*Shaiva Agamas*
Jagat	Shakta	Shakti	Tantra	*Devi Bhagavata*

"O foolish mind, stop your fearful fretting about the extensive torments imposed by the god of death. How can your enemies, the karmic reactions you have accrued, even touch you? After all, is your master not the Supreme Lord Narayana, the husband of Goddess Sri Lakshmi? Cast aside all hesitation and concentrate your thoughts on Lord Narayana, whom one very easily attains through devotional consciousness. What can that dispeller of the whole world's troubles not do for His own serv-

---

[10] The Prasthana Traya is a collection of three scriptures: a) the *Upanishads*, b) the *Bhagavad Gita*, and c) the *Brahma Sutras*.

56

ant?" (*Mukunda-Mala-Stotra*, 10)

"Narayana is the eye as well as the visible, ear as well as the audible, nose and scent, tongue and taste, skin and the tactile, mind and the thinkable, intellect and its contents, ego and its field, speech and its contents, hands, feet, their fields, evacuation and production – all are Narayana. Supporter, ordainer, transformer – all is He." (*Subala Upanishad*, 3:2-3)

"There is no room for performing *puja* (worship of deities), *namaskaram* (paying homage with prostration), *japa* (recitation of *mantras*), *dhyana* (meditation), and so on. Hear from me that the highest truth acclaimed in the *Vedas* can be known only through *jnana*; hence, there is absolutely no need to know anything outside of oneself." (Lord Shiva explaining his path to his consort Parvati in the *Devikalottara Agama*, 17)

"'With offerings I propitiate the branches of this swift-moving God, the bounteous Vishnu.' Hence Rudra (Shiva) gained his Rudra-strength." (*Rig Veda*, 7.40.5)

"Even while engaging his senses in contact with their objects, one who sees this whole world as the energy of Sri Vishnu is neither repelled nor elated. He is indeed the greatest among devotees." (*Srimad Bhagavatam*, 11.2.48)

Question: What are you seeking as your ultimate spiritual goal?

A) God, the Divine

B) Self-understanding, Self-realization

C) Mastery over subtle energies and internal powers

In accordance with your answer, which of the three paths should you be following?[11]

Chapter 5 Ontology: Human Person, God and Creation

The Tri-Tattva, or Three Reals, concept is a very important Vedic principle to understand. For this reason, we go into much greater depth and detail in our exploration of the Three Reals of Vedic philosophy in chapter five. We do this by discussing a) the human person, b) God, and c) the Creation, which corresponds with 1) Atman, 2) Brahman, and 3) Jagat, respectively.

5.1.1 A) THE HUMAN PERSON

The human person is much more than merely a physical being, as Atheists claim. He is also more than merely a physical being with a mind, as many Western philosophers claim. Rather, he is a multi-dimensional being, with *atman* constituting his most important aspect and his true self. The various elements of the human person are seen in the following qualitative hierarchy, with the most superior and subtlest element at the top, and progressing into increasing degrees of qualitative inferiority and denseness as we proceed down the list. Above the human person is the Parama-Purusha, or Supreme Person, God.

---

[11] If (A), then you are a Vaishnava. If (B), then you are a Shaiva. If (C), then you are a Shakta. If your answer is that you wish to have all three, then the path you should follow is Vaishnavism, because, in having the very highest of all, you have everything.

GOD

(Source of the Human Person)

ELEMENTS OF THE HUMAN PERSON

Consciousness (*atman*)

Illusory Ego (*ahamkara*)

Intellect (*buddhi*)

Mind (*manas*)

Emotions (*abhitapa*)

Body (*deha*)

"The Supreme Lord manifested the material intelligence, senses, mind, and vital air (*prana*) of the living entities so that they could indulge their desires for sense gratification, take repeated births to engage in fruitive activities, become elevated in future lives, and ultimately attain liberation." (*Srimad Bhagavatam*, 10.87.2)

"Beyond the senses are the objects. Beyond the objects is the mind. Beyond the mind, there is the intellect. Beyond the intellect, there is the great *atman*. Beyond the great *atman*, there is the Unmanifest. Beyond the Unmanifest, there is the Supreme Godhead. Beyond the Supreme Godhead there is nothing. This is the end, the Supreme Goal." (*Katha Upanishad*, 1.3.10-11)

Questions: We know our body is impermanent. But is our mind impermanent? Have you ever changed your mind? Is your intellect impermanent? Has your intelligence ever grown in your lifetime? What about emotions? When you feel angry, sad or elated, do these feelings last forever? Or are they merely fleeting and temporary?

5.1.2 Atman

It is specifically the *atman*, our consciousness, that is the truly spiritual element of the human person. *Atman* is the true, eternal self. Sometimes the *atman* is referred to as spirit, or soul in the West. Since God is the source of each and every *atman*, the *atman* shares in the many positive qualities of God. Thus, the *atman* is non-distinct from God in quality (i.e., both are essentially consciousness), but it is different from God in quantity. *Atman* is the effect and God is the Source of that effect. The *atman* is finite, but God is infinite. The *atman* is dependent upon God, but God is dependent upon nothing. The *atman* possesses the possibility of falling into illusion, but God never falls under illusion. God is the master of illusion. We are *atman* (true self), but God is Paramatman (the Supreme Self).

> *eso 'nur atma cetasa veditavyo*
> *yasmin pranah pancadha samvivesa*
> *pranais cittam sarvam otam prajanam*
> *yasmin visuddhe vibhavaty esa atma*

"The soul is atomic in size and can be perceived by perfect intelligence. This atomic soul is floating in the five kinds of air (*prana, apana, vyana, samana* and *udana*), is situated within the heart, and spreads its influence all over the body of the embodied living entities. When the soul is purified from the contamination of the five kinds of material air, its spiritual influence is exhibited." (*Mundaka Upanishad*, 3.1.9)

> *balagra-sata-bhagasya*
> *satadha kalpitasya cha*
> *bhago jivah vijneyah*
> *sa chanantyaya kalpate*

"When the upper point of a hair is divided into one hundred parts and again each of such parts is further divided into one hundred parts, each such part is the measurement of the dimension of the spirit soul." (*Shvet-asvatara Upanishad*, 5.9)

"The Supreme within the heart is the size of a thumb and is like light without smoke." (*Taittiriya Upanishad*, 4.13)[12]

> *avinasi tu tad viddhi yena sarvam idam tatam*
> *vinasham avyayasyasya na kaschit kartum arhati*

"Know that which pervades the entire body is indestructible. No one is able to destroy the imperishable soul." (*Bhagavad Gita*, 2.17)

> *na jayate mriyate va kadachin*
> *nayam bhutva bhavita va na bhuyah*
> *ajo nityah sasvato 'yam purano*
> *na hanyate hanyamane sharire*

"For the soul there is never birth nor death. Nor, having once been, does he ever cease to be. He is unborn, eternal, ever-existing, undying and primeval. He is not slain when the body is slain." (*Bhagavad Gita*, 2.20)

"This self is fourfold: the self of waking who has the outer intelligence and enjoys external things, is its first part; the self of dream who has the inner intelligence and enjoys subtle things is its second part; the self of sleep, unified, a massed intelligence, blissful and enjoying, is the third part; the controller of all the lower elements, the knower, the inner consciousness. That which is unseen, indefinable, self-evident in its selfhood, is the fourth part: this is the self (*atman*), this is that which has to be known." (*Mandukya Upanishad*, 2-7)

---

[12] When we compare this verse from the *Taittiriya Upanishad* to the verse above it from the *Shvetashvatara Upanishad*, it is clear that the Vedic scriptures make an unequivocal distinction between our own soul, the *atman*, and God as He is present within our heart, the Paramatman. *Atman* and Paramatman are united in their ontological make up, in that they are both of the nature of consciousness, but they are distinct in that Paramatman is the Source, and the individual *atman* is the effect that is derived from that Source. God is God, and you are you, and eternally so.

<u>Questions</u> : What are several positive and auspicious attributes that we can think of? For example, beauty, kindness, etc. Those positive attributes that you have discovered in yourself all have your *atman* as their source.

What is the Source of your *atman?*

5.1.3 Aham-pratyaya vs. Aham-kara: I-Cognition vs. Illusory Ego

There are two very different senses of identity, or cognizance of "I-ness", that the *atman* can chose to experience.

1) *Aham-pratyaya*: I-cognition

2) *Aham-kara*: I-maker

Aham-pratyaya (I-cognition) is our natural sense of selfhood, individuality, or I-ness. This is the purely spiritual sense of "I" in relation to all other things in our environment and to God. Thus, it is a positive and healthy sense of "I". *Aham-pratyaya* is pure, spiritual identity.

Aham-kara (literally "I-maker"), on the other hand, is an artificial and illusory sense of selfhood. It is the false "I" that occurs when we mistakenly identify with that which is not the true self, such as our body, our false persona, our ethnicity, gender, age, etc. Another term for *aham-kara* is false ego. The *yogi* seeks to transcend false ego (*aham-kara*) and to re-embrace his true, spiritual self (*aham-pratyaya*).

"To dwell in our true being is liberation; the sense of false ego is a fall from the truth of our being." (*Maha Upanishad*, 5.2)

62

Questions: How are we not the body? Or the emotions? Or the Mind? Or the intellect? What aspect of us is always there, even though all of these lower aspects change, come and go?

When we have transcended our false sense of self, what is then left?

5.1.4 Inherent Individuality of the Atman

Vedic spirituality teaches that each and every single *atman* is a unique and singular individual. This is true of both the infinite number of dependent *atmans*, but of God as well. We do not lose our individual sense of self upon liberation. Our identity is not merely "merged" into God, or some impersonal energy, to be forever lost. Rather, upon liberation, we re-member and re-embrace our true and eternal identity as a purely spiritual being, and enjoy eternity in loving and reciprocal loving relationship with God. Individuality is an inherent aspect of our very souls.

Nityo nityanam chetanas chetananam
eko bahunam vidadhati kaman

"That Supreme Godhead is one, and the living creatures are many, many, without any number." (*Katha Upanishad*, 2.2.13)

Question: What is your earliest memory of realizing that your sense of self was distinct from everything and everyone else around you?

5.1.5 Consciousness and Personality

All living beings have personality. Personality is an inherent aspect of
both God and of all individual souls. Personality, in fact, is non-different
from consciousness. Everything that has consciousness has personality,
and everything that has personality has consciousness. We know that
consciousness and personality are the same thing because both consciousness and personality share the exact same essential attributes. The
four primary essential attributes that both personality and consciousness
must have in order to exist and function are:

A) Free-will

B) Self-awareness

C) Awareness/knowledge of things external to oneself

D) A natural propensity to seek and experience joy

What we are meant to transcend is our present, artificial personality that
has come about as a direct result of ego (*ahamkara*), while fully embracing
our true, spiritual personality that is an expression of our consciousness.

"I worship that transcendental seat, known as Shvetadvipa where as loving consorts the Lakshmis in their unalloyed spiritual essence practice the
loving service of the Supreme Lord Narayana as their only love; where
every tree is a transcendental purpose tree; where the soil is the purpose
gem, all water is nectar, every word is a song, every gait is a dance, the
flute is the favorite attendant, effulgence is full of transcendental bliss
and the supreme spiritual entities are all enjoyable and tasty, where num-
berless milk cows always emit transcendental oceans of milk; where there
is eternal existence of transcendental time, who is ever present and without past or future and hence is not subject to the quality of passing away
even for the space of half a moment. That realm is known as Goloka
only to a very few self-realized souls in this world." (*Brahma Samhita*,
5.56)

"In the Vaikuntha realm (the highest spiritual realm), all the residents are similar in form to the Supreme Godhead, Vishnu. It is their Dharma to all engage in worship of the Lord without desires for sense gratification." (*Srimad Bhagavatam*, 3.15.14)

"In the Vaikuntha planets the inhabitants fly in their airplanes, accompanied by their wives and consorts, and eternally sing of the character and activities of the Lord, which are always devoid of all inauspicious qualities. While singing the glories of the Lord, they deride even the presence of the blossoming madhavi flowers, which are fragrant and laden with honey." (*Srimad Bhagavatam*, 3.15.17)

Questions: What would our existence be like if we did not have the four essential attributes of personality/consciousness? What would we be if we did not have will, self-awareness, the ability to know anything, and the experience of joy?

What would it mean to deprive God of these essential attributes of personality/consciousness?

5.2.1 Equality of Spirit and Hierarchy of Form

No two things in this world are equal and the same. If they were, then they would occupy the same space, time, ontological makeup and identity. Similarly, no two human beings in existence are the same. We are all different from one another, both in identity and in inherent qualities. To state otherwise would be to limit God's infinite creativity and to reduce each living being to a state of amorphous monotony devoid of freedom and inherent dignity. Equality, in any real sense other than legal status, does not exist in the material world. It is only in the realm of consciousness that we can talk about true substantial equality. We are all equal in the eyes of God, and through the vision of pure consciousness.

"Every person should act like this: when he meets a person more qualified than himself, he should be very pleased; when he meets someone
less qualified than himself, he should be compassionate toward him; and
when he meets someone of similar station to himself, he should make
friendship with him. In this way one is never affected by the threefold
miseries of the material world." (*Srimad Bhagavatam*, 4.8.34)

ya nisha sarva-bhutanam tasyam jagarti samyami
yasyam jagrati bhutani sa nisha pashyato muneh

"What is night for all beings is the time of awakening for the self-
controlled; and the time of awakening for all beings is night for the intro-
spective sage." (*Bhagavad Gita*, 2.69)

Vidya-vinaya-sampanne brahmane gavi hastini
Shuni chaiva shvapake cha panditah sama-darshinah

"The humble sage, by virtue of true knowledge, sees with equal vision
[*sama-darshina*] the learned and gentle priest, a cow, an elephant, a dog or
an outcaste." (*Bhagavad Gita*, 18.5)

Sri-havir uvacha
sarva-bhutesu yah pashyed bhagavad-bhavam atmanah
bhutani bhagavaty atmany esha bhagavatottamah

"Sri Havir said: The most advanced devotee sees within everything the
soul of all souls, the Supreme Godhead, Sri Krishna. Consequently he
sees everything in relation to the Supreme Lord and understands that
everything that exists is eternally situated within the Lord." (*Srimad Bhagavatam*, 11.2.45)

Questions: What natural characteristics, talents and skills do have
that you don't often observe in most others? What characteristics, talents and skills do you wish you had that you see in
others?

5.2.2 Varna: Understanding Your Psychophysical Nature

In order to better understand our own individual psychological and physical natures, along with our particular likes and dislikes, preferences,
natural talents, motivations, etc., the *rishis* (seer-sages) devised an ingen-
ious system of human categorization, known as *varna*. The *varna* system
outlines four psychophysical categories that most human individuals fall
under and operate from. These four *varnas* are:

Brahmanas: Intellectuals, philosophers, teachers, priests.

Kshatriyas: Warriors, administrators, managers, political leaders.

Vaishyas: Merchants, farmers, cattlemen, producers.

Shudras: Laborers, craftsmen, hands-on technicians, medical
surgeons.

Through the process of self-examination and determining into which of
these four *varnas* our personalities feel most at home, we have the ability
to know ourselves much better, and to unleash our inner creative poten-
tial in alliance with our inherent nature.

"*Brahmanas, kshatriyas, vaishyas* and *shudras* are distinguished by the qualities arising from their own natures in accordance with the material
modes, O chastiser of the enemy." (*Bhagavad Gita*, 18.41)

"Purity (external and internal), performance of virtuous deeds, abstaining
from actions that hurt one's body excessively, absence of ill-will towards
everyone, absence of hatred, control of the senses, charity and compassion – these are the characteristics of the *brahmana*." (*Atri Samhita*, 1.33)

"Let a *brahmana*, after having examined all these worlds that are gained by works, acquire freedom from desires; nothing that is eternal can be produced by what is not eternal. In order that he may understand that eternal, let him, fuel in hand, approach a *guru* who is well versed in the *Vedas* and always devoted to God (Brahman). (*Mundaka Upanishad,* 1.2.12)

"Peacefulness, self-control, austerity, purity, tolerance, honesty, knowledge, wisdom and religiousness - these are the natural qualities by which the *brahmanas* work." (*Bhagavad Gita,* 18.42)

"Heroism, power, determination, resourcefulness, courage in battle, generosity and leadership are the natural qualities of work for the *kshatriyas.*" (*Bhagavad Gita,* 18.43)

"Farming, cow protection and business are the natural work for the *vaishyas,* and for the *shudras* there is labor and service to others." (*Bhagavad Gita,* 18.44)

"It is far better to honor one's own nature (*sva-dharma*), even though faultily, than to perform another's duties perfectly. Destruction in the course of honoring one's own nature is better than engaging in another's duties, for to follow another's path is dangerous." (*Bhagavad Gita,* 3.35)

Exercise: Please choose among the following options to gain a clearer idea of which *varna* most expresses your psychophysical nature:

1. I enjoy:
   a) Reading
   b) Boxing and martial arts
   c) Playing the stock market
   d) Working on my car

2. My favorite foods include:
   a) Organic, healthy and vegetarian
   b) Food I hunt myself

c) Inexpensive food grown on my family farm

d) Greasy and non-vegetarian fast-food

3. I use my mind to:
   a) Think of philosophical and scholarly matters
   b) Think of strategies, politics and logically ordering social structures (any human grouping ranging from an office to a nation)
   c) Producing the maximal degree of abundance at the minimal amount of cost or energy expenditure
   d) I prefer to use my hands rather than think

4. For entertainment and relaxation I:
   a) Enjoy reading and taking walks deep in nature
   b) Like watching/participating in competitive sports
   c) Going to expensive restaurants and networking at parties
   d) Going to bars, tail-gating and barbeques

5. The end justifies the means:
   a) Never
   b) Only if it benefits a greater cause
   c) Almost always in business practices
   d) Yes

'A' answers indicate a *brahmana* nature.

'B' answers indicate a *kshatriya* nature.

'C' answers indicate a *vaishya* nature.

'D' answers indicate a *shudra* nature.

The letter that you picked the most times shows your specific predilection toward one of these four psychophysical natures.

Guidance: There is sometimes an overlap between conjoining *varnas*. A person can be a *brahmana-kshatriya*, or a *kshatriya-vaishya*, or a *vaishya-shudra*. But such overlapping never skips a *varna*. In other words, there is no such thing as a *brahmana-shudra*, etc. Finally, *varnas* are fluid within a person's lifetime. A person's *varna* can gradually change.

5.2.3 The Three Personality Types

Human personalities are not all the same. We are not all equal in our behavior, motivations, spiritual attainment, or moral outlook. Vedic
philosophy places people into three distinct personality types, all three of
which fall into a larger spectrum of individuals that make up any given
society.

On one side of this spectrum are a small minority of people who are
what the *Bhagavad Gita* terms *daivika*, or inherently good and spiritual. On
the extreme opposite side of the spectrum, we have a small minority of
persons who are considered *asurika*, or inherently psychopathic and atheistic in nature. The vast majority of people fall somewhere in the middle
of the spectrum, and are called *laukika*, or innocent and common-folk. It
is in our spiritual interest to know which of these three personality types
we are, and how to relate to others in accordance with their own personality types.

Daivika   Common   Asurika

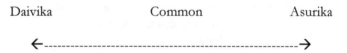

Ideally, we will desire to be of *daivika* nature, and to associate with
friends and family who are also daivika. We will be very conscious to
avoid those of *asurika* nature at all costs, or else they will drag us down to
their unhappy level. And we will compassionately help the *laukikas* to
elevate themselves spiritually.

dambho darpo 'bhimanas cha krodhah parushyam eva cha
ajnanam chabhijatasya partha sampadam asurim

"Arrogance, pride, anger, conceit, harshness and ignorance - these qualities belong to those of demonic nature (*asuras*), O son of Prtha."
(*Bhagavad Gita*, 16.4)

"Both gods and demons come from Prajapati. The arrogant demons asked, 'To whom should we offer?' They placed the offerings into their own mouths, and through arrogance they were overcome. Therefore no one should be arrogant. Arrogance is indeed the source of destruction. The gods then proceeded to place their oblations each in the mouth of one of his fellows. And Prajapati gave himself over to them. In this way the gods became owners of sacrifice, for sacrifice is really the food of the gods." (*Shatapatha Brahmana*, 5.1.1.1-2)

"As long as one does not inquire about the spiritual values of life, one is defeated and subjected to miseries arising from ignorance. Be it wrongful or meritorious, all material action has its resultant actions. If a person is engaged in any kind of material activity, his mind is called *karmatmaka*, colored with fruitive activity. As long as the mind is impure, consciousness is unclear, and as long as one is absorbed in fruitive activity, he has to accept a material body." (*Srimad Bhagavatam*, 5.5.5)

Exercise: Which of the following two lists do you most identify with? Or do you identify with a pretty much equal number of items from both columns?

Daivika Nature	**Asurika Nature**
Humility	Glib and superficial
Cleanliness	Self-centered
Ethical	Narcissistic
Steadiness	No moral inhibitions
Self-control	Needs constant stimulation
Even-mindedness	Lies effortlessly
Devotion to God	Exploits others' sympathy
Austere	Targets naïve people
Detached from materialism	Enjoys abusing living beings
Wise	Parasitical
Healthy in body and mind	Feels no remorse
Seeks good and light	Seeks sinister and darkness
Honorable	Enjoys humiliating others
Trustworthy	Overly sexualized behavior
Loyal	Atheistic
Compassionate	Manipulative
Reveres beauty	Exploits beauty
Loving	Cynical
Speaks the truth	Worships dark beings

Which of these two columns most reflects your own inner nature? If you wish to know and live a life of truth, then cultivate the *daivika* qualities and abandon the *asurika* qualities.

5.3.1 Karma and Reincarnation

The Sanskrit word *"karma"* simply means action. But those actions that are performed by human beings with the specific purpose of either hurting or benefiting other living beings also produce a direct reaction toward the performer of such actions. This is recompensatory *karma*, or *karma* as a direct consequence of our actions. The process of reincarnation is completely dependent upon the cosmic law of *karma*, since it is *karma* that determines how and why we reincarnate into future bodies. *Karma* is the cause, and reincarnation is the effect. So, there is no reincarnation without *karma*; and if there is *karma*, there must be reincarnation. The two principles are inseparable. The cause of all *karma*, however, is our own free will choices. We, and only we, create our own *karma*. The goal of Sanatana Dharma and Yoga is to transcend all karmic activity, thus achieving liberation (*moksha*).

"By means of desires, contact, attachment and delusion, the embodied soul assumes, successively, diverse forms in various places, according to its deeds, just as the body grows when food and drink are poured into it. The embodied soul, by means of good and evil deeds committed by itself, assumes many forms, coarse and fine. By virtue of its actions and also of such characteristics of the mind as knowledge and desire, it assumes another body for the enjoyment of suitable objects. He who knows the Lord, who is without beginning or end, who stands in the midst of the chaos of the world, who is the ultimate Creator of all things and is endowed with many forms - he who knows the radiant Deity, the sole Pervader of the universe, is released from all his fetters." (*Shvetashvatara Upanishad*, 5:11-13)

"After many births and deaths, he who is actually in knowledge surrenders unto Me, knowing Me to be the cause of all causes and all that is. Such a great soul is very rare." (Sri Krishna, *Bhagavad Gita*, 7:19)

"Birth and other transformations are undergone by the body, but never by the self, just as change occurs for the moon's phases but never for the moon, though the new-moon day may be called the moon's "death.""
(*Srimad Bhagavatam*, 10.54.47)

> <u>Fact</u>: Many people tend to fantasize about having been a famous person in a previous life – George Washington, Queen Cleopat ra, Alexander the Great, or some other heroic figure. According to the Vedic scriptures, however, there are 8,400,000 species of life, any one of which we may have been in our previous life. We may have been an ant or a god in our last life. There are 400,000 different species of human beings alone, and a wide variety of classes, socio-economic groupings, and situations that humans find themselves in. The odds that we were a famous king or queen in our last few lives is not as likely as the possibility that we were probably a peasant or servant. More, there are multiple universes in which we may have lived in a previous life. Knowing this, it is more important to try to free ourselves from the cycle of reincarnation altogether rather than romanticize about who we may have been in a previous life.

5.3.2 Karma and Fatalism

It is an incorrect stereotype to believe that the principle of *karma* is the same as believing in fate. *Karma* has nothing to do with fate or a lack of free will. On the contrary, the principle of *karma* teaches us that we have the freedom to create our own future through our present actions, even extending into many lifetimes from now. We freely create our own futures – whether good or bad. *Karma* is a principle of freedom, and Sanatana Dharma is a path of freedom. So, let us use that freedom wisely, and choose to know our true self and to know God.

yam yam vapi smaran bhavam tyajaty ante kalevaram
tam tam evaiti kaunteya sada tad-bhava-bhavitah

74

"Whatever state of being one remembers when he quits his body, that state he will attain without fail." (*Bhagavad Gita*, 8.6)

"We live in accordance with our deep, driving desire. It is this desire at the time of death that determines what our next life will be. We will come back to earth to work out the satisfaction of that desire. But not for those who are free from desire; they are free because all their desires have been fulfilled in the Absolute. They do not die like the others; but realizing Brahman, they come to know Brahman. So it is said: 'When all material desires that surge in the heart are renounced, the mortal becomes immortal. When all the knots that strangle the heart are loosened, the mortal becomes immortal, here in this very life.'" (*Brihadaranyaka Upanishad*, 4.4.6-7)

"He who desires the world of the ancestors, by his mere will the ancestors come to receive him, and having obtained the world of the ancestors he is happy, etc. Whatever object he is attached to, whatever object he desires, by his mere will it comes to him, and having obtained it he is happy." (*Chandogya Upanishad*, 8:2)

"Living beings entangled in the complicated meshes of birth and death can be freed at once by even unconsciously chanting the holy name of Krishna, which is feared by fear personified." (*Srimad Bhagavatam*, 1.1.14)

"The Supreme Lord manifested the material intelligence, senses, mind, and vital air of the living beings so that they could indulge their desires for sense gratification, take repeated births to engage in fruitive activities, become elevated in future lives, and ultimately attain liberation." (*Srimad Bhagavatam* 10.87.2)

Question: If you freely choose to jump off a cliff, was it merely fate that you eventually hit the ground, or was it the immediate result of *karma* that was put into motion due to your own decision to jump?
Contemplation: Freedom is more of an internal state of consciousness than just an external ability to perform specific acts of one's choosing. If a person has wealth and power, but uses those

means only to harm others, then he is a slave of his ego. He is in bondage. On the other hand, if a person has only a little wealth, but chooses not to steal from those less fortunate than him, he is the master of his actions. He is free.

5.3.3 Refuting the Theory of Collective Karma

As spiritual beings, we are all unique individuals, with our own inherent free will, karmic history, personalities and futures. Due to our inherent freedom as individuals, the karmic prospects of one person cannot be necessarily tied to the karmic prospects of a collective of individuals. All of the individuals of a given group cannot share one *karma*. Each person, in other words, only experiences his own *karma* that he produced, and not the *karma* of someone else. To be forced to experience the *karma* of some other person's actions would be the equivalent of sentencing person A for the crimes of person B. That would make the universe unjust, which it is not. All living beings are one in the sense that we are all qualitatively consciousness in our essence. But we are all different in that our individual wills (*sankalpa*) are exclusive to each of us as independent beings. I have my *karma*, and you have yours.

"Here they say that a person consists of desires. And as is his desire, so is his will. As is his will, so is his deed. Whatever deed he does, that he will reap." (*Brihadaranyaka Upanishad*, 4.4.5)

"He who, cherishing objects, desires those objects, is born again here or there through his desires. But for him whose desires are satisfied and who is established in the *atman*, all desires vanish even here on earth." (*Mundaka Upanishad*, 3.2.2)

Questions: How strong is your will? Is your will currently a reflection of the inherent goodness of your true self, or of the illusion of ego?

Exercise: A strong and healthy will can be developed by almost anyone. Whenever faced with a clear choice between a lazy course of action (for example, sitting and vegetating in front of the TV.) versus a course that will lead to some form of self-improvement (for example, reading an inspiring book or getting some exercise), consciously and purposefully use your power of will to choose the path of self-improvement. With continuous practice, you will develop an increasingly stronger and healthier power of will.

5.3.4 Is There "Evidence" for Reincarnation and Karma?

Metaphysical principles and realities cannot be "proven" in the same sense as physical principles and objects can be proven. This is the case because metaphysical realities operate outside the bounds of the material. Thus, the metaphysical cannot be detected via the material. However, we can infer the necessary existence of such metaphysical principles as Dharma, time, *karma* and reincarnation. Without the very real existence of the two principles of *karma* and reincarnation, for example, there is no philosophical answer available to us to the question of the origins of suffering in the world. Unlike any other philosophical or theological system in the world, the doctrine of *karma*/reincarnation provides completely satisfying answers to the existence of suffering.[13]

"The eye does not go there, nor speech, nor the mind. We do not know It. We do not understand how anyone can teach It. It is different from the known. It is above the unknown. Thus we have heard from the pre-

---

[13] Max Weber considered the principle of *karma* to be "the most consistent theodicy ever produced." Quoted from Matilal, B. K. The Collected Essays of Bimal Krishna Matilal: Ethics and Epics. Pg. 39. New Delhi, 2002.

ceptors of old who taught It to us." (*Kena Upanishad*, 1.3-4)

> Question: What things are there that you and everyone else
> know as an undeniable fact are very real, but the existence of
> which cannot be proven by any sense detection or via the scien-
> tific method?

> Fact: God is all good, all-powerful, and all-knowing. Without the
> principle of *karma* and reincarnation to explain the presence of
> suffering in the world, suffering can only be explained if we re-
> move one of these qualities from God.

5.4.1 Discerning Spirit from Matter

In the process of self-realization, knowing what we are and knowing
what we are not, are two important sides of the same process of realization of our true self. Through the process of Jnana Yoga, we are
equipped with the necessary philosophical tools to distinguish between
our true and eternal self versus anything that is not related to that true
self. The most general of these divisions is the distinction that exists between consciousness (*atman*) and materiality (*prakriti*). The soul is eternal
(*nitya*), but anything material is temporary (*anitya*). The soul is animate
(*ajada*), but all material things are inanimate (*jada*). The soul is sentient
(*chetana*), but material things are insentient (*achetana*). The discipline of
Jnana Yoga, or the Yoga of discernment, is especially equipped to help us
make such crucial distinctions.[14]

---

[14] The distinction between matter and spirit is only one of the preliminary goals
of Jnana Yoga. The other goals are the cultivation of rational and logical analytical abilities, with the ultimate goal of awakening one's innate *buddhi*, or wisdom-
faculty.

na tv evaham jatu nasham na tvam neme janadhipah
na chaiva na bhavishyamah sarve vayam atah param

"Never was there a time when I did not exist, nor you, nor all these kings; nor in the future shall any of us cease to be." (*Bhagavad Gita*, 2.12)

dehino 'smin yatha dehe kaumaram yauvanam jara
tatha dehantara-praptir dhiras tatra na muhyati

"As the embodied soul continuously passes, in this body, from boyhood to youth to old age, the soul similarly passes into another body at death. A self-realized soul is not bewildered by such a change." (*Bhagavad Gita*, 2.13)

matra-sparshas tu kaunteya sitoshna-sukha-duhkha-dah
agamapayino 'nityas tams titikshasva bharata

"O son of Kunti, the nonpermanent appearance of happiness and distress, and their disappearance in due course, are like the appearance and disappearance of winter and summer seasons. They arise from sense perception, O scion of Bharata (Arjuna), and one must learn to tolerate them without being disturbed." (*Bhagavad Gita*, 2.14)

na hi jnanena sadrsham pavitram iha vidyate
tat svayam yoga-samsiddhah kalenatmani vindati

"In this world, there is nothing so sublime and pure as transcendental knowledge. Such knowledge is the mature fruit of all Yoga..." (*Bhagavad Gita*, 4:38).

nashato vidyate bhavo nabhavo vidyate satah
ubhayor api drshto'ntas tv anayos tattva-darshibhih

"Those who are seers of the truth (*tattva-darshibhih*) have concluded that of the nonexistent (matter) there is no endurance, and of the existent (consciousness) there is no cessation. This seers have concluded by studying the nature of both" (*Bhagavad Gita*, 2:16)

Questions: When you are seeing an object using your eye, is it the eye itself that is seeing, or is it you seeing through your eye? Is it the ear that is hearing, or is it you hearing through your ear?

When you are seated in meditation and you begin to observe the chattering of your mind, who is observing your mind?

5.5.1 B) God: The Nature of the Absolute.

To remind the reader, there are three ultimate Reals in Vedic philosophy. These three Reals (called the Tri-Tattva in Sanskrit) are Atman (individual units of consciousness), Brahman (the Absolute, who is the source of Atman and Jagat) and Jagat (all non-sentient materiality). In this second section of chapter five of the book *Sanatana Dharma: The Eternal Natural Way*, we look much deeper into specific issues involved in understanding the nature of Brahman (God).

"Now, then, is the time to inquire into the nature of Brahman." (*Brahma Sutras*, 1.1.1)

5.5.2 Brahman is not Anthropomorphic "God"

The Vedic concept of God is very different from the Abrahamic concept of "God". The Abrahamic religions have an anthropomorphic concept. In other words, their vision of the nature of God is very much a reflection of their own flawed, human personalities. Thus, the being described in the Old Testament and the *Qur'an* tends to have very human-like emotions and motivations. He gets angry, is jealous, territorial, violently aggressive, and demands that we fear him.

For Sanatana Dharma, on the other hand, God (Brahman) is not seen as being merely a reflection of flawed human beings. Rather, we are a reflection of God. God is the infinite Source of the finite. God is the possessor and Source of an infinite number of auspicious qualities expanded to their infinitely maximal degree. God is perfect goodness, beauty, truth, eternality, compassion, power, etc.

"He is without hands and feet, and yet He moves and grasps. He sees, though without eyes. He hears, though without ears. He knows whatever is to be known, and of Him there is no knower. They speak of Him as the first, the Supreme Person (*purusham mahantam*)." (*Shvetashvatara Upanishad*, 3.19)

"There is nothing beyond the Supreme One (*tatah param*)." (*Atharva Veda*, 7.50.8)

> Question: What would be some of the disadvantages to God if God were suddenly possessed of human qualities?

> Fact: God is that person than which nothing greater can be conceived. So, whatever is the maximum degree of goodness, beauty, etc. that we can imagine, God is greater than even that.

5.5.3 What is Brahman?

The concept of God as understood in the Vedic tradition is very different from the idea of God that has been taught in recent centuries in the West. Here we begin to explore the inner nature of God, including some of the infinite attributes of the Divine. Three of these attributes, for example, are truth, knowledge and infinity. Brahman transcends the entire material cosmos, yet is present within all things that are a part of the material cosmos.

satyam jnanam anantam brahma

"Brahman is of the nature of truth, knowledge and infinity." (*Taittiriya Upanishad*, 2.1.1)

"God is the inner, sinless, Supreme Self, the divine Narayana." (*Subala Upanishad*, 4:1)

"My dear Uddhava, I am the cause, protector and the Lord of all mystic perfections, of the Yoga system, of analytical knowledge, of pure activity and of the community of learned Vedic teachers. Just as the same material elements exist within and outside of all material bodies, similarly, I cannot be covered by anything else. I exist within everything as the Paramatman and outside of everything in My all-pervading feature." (Sri Krishna, *Srimad Bhagavatam*, 11.15.35-36)

Questions: What do you envision when you hear the term "God"?

When you hear the term "God", do you think of something you are meant to fear or to love?

Fact: The concept of God as the all-good Source of all reality existed within the tradition of Sanatana Dharma for thousands of years before any similar concepts appeared in other religions. God was known to the ancient *rishis* (seer-sages) thousands of years before Moses. The concept of God is first found in the *Rig Veda* (circa 3800 BCE), which is recognized by all scholars as the most ancient human writing in Earth's history. But it existed in Sanatana Dharma before it was even first written down.

5.5.4 Does God Have Attributes?

Because God does not have material attributes of any kind (for example, a physical body, a specific height and size that can be measured in space, an age that can be measured in time, etc.), some writers in the past have

82

made the mistake of thinking that God must not have any sort of attributes at all. The Vedic scriptures do teach that God does not have physical attributes. At the same time, however, the Vedic scriptures do <u>not</u> teach that God is devoid of spiritual attributes. Indeed, God is defined as *ananta-kalyana-gunaih*; He is the possessor of an infinite number of auspicious attributes. These infinite auspicious attributes are all spiritual in nature, thus they are not limited, they are perfect, and they are all inherently good.

There are two philosophical terms that have often confused practitioners of Sanatana Dharma. These two terms are:

> **Nirguna**: meaning that Brahman transcends all material attributes.
> **Saguna**: meaning that Brahman has infinite auspicious attributes.

Previous confusion came from the mistaken idea that God is necessarily one or the other. That He either has attributes, or that He does not. In actuality, the Vedic scriptures make it quite clear that the terms *nirguna* and *saguna* are not mutually exclusive terms in relation to Brahman. Rather, God is both *nirguna* and *saguna* simultaneously. He does not have any material attributes, but does possess infinite auspicious attributes that are wholly spiritual in nature. Indeed, both the qualities of *nirguna* and *saguna* themselves are descriptive attributes of the Divine. The full nature of God's attributes is beyond our conception, but not beyond our experience.

"When the Vedic literature describes the Supreme Godhead as being without any qualities (*nirguna*), this means that the Lord does not possess any material qualities. It does not mean that he has no spiritual qualities." (*Padma Purana, Uttara Khanda* 255.39.40)

"Now, therefore, the description of Brahman: 'Not this, not this'; for there is no other and more appropriate description than this 'Not this.' Now the designation of Brahman: 'The Truth of truth.' The vital breath is truth, and Brahman is the Truth of that. (*Brihadaranyaka Upanishad,* 2.3.6)

"Everywhere are His hands and legs, His eyes and faces, and He hears everything. In this way Brahman exists." (*Bhagavad Gita,* 13.14)

prajnanam brahma

"Brahman is consciousness." (*Aitareya Upanishad,* 3.1.3)

"Brahman is bliss." (*Taittiriya Upanishad,* 3.6.1)

> Exercise: Think of every positive attributive quality that you can. Some examples include: beauty, kindness, strength, intelligence, truth, majesty, splendor, brilliance, etc. Now try to envision these attributes to an infinite qualitative and powerful degree. Contemplate the fact that such infinite positive attributes have Brahman (God) as their very source. Now meditate upon that Source with great devotion.

5.5.5 The Nature of Brahman

Overflowing abundance is one of the auspicious attributes of Brahman. The term "Brahman" itself comes from the Sanskrit verb root "*brh*", which means "to grow". It is the nature of Brahman to ever-increase His infinite grandeur and creative outpouring. Brahman is that from which all good things proceed. Thus He is especially known as the *jagat-karana,* or the cause of the material world. He is also known as the *karana-karanam,* the cause of all causes. God is the cosmogonal source of all spiritual and

84

material realities.

Janmad yasya yatah

"Brahman is that from which all creation proceeds." (*Brahma Sutras*, 1.1.2)

Sarvam khalv idam brahma

"All this that we see in the world is Brahman." (*Chandogya Upanishad*, 3.14.1)

"Brahman thought: 'May I be many; may I grow forth'." (*Chandogya Upanishad*, 6:2:3)

> Exercise: Think of any particular thing in existence, either a real object that you can perceive with your senses or something that you can conceive with your mind. What is the immediate cause of that object? What is the immediate cause of that cause? Follow the chain of causality in your mind until you can no longer go back any further. The ultimate end point, the cause of all causes is Brahman. Now meditate upon Brahman with devotion in order to know that cause of all causes.

5.5.6 God and Determinism

The material creation comes about as a direct result of individual souls (*atmans*) falling into illusion, and thus needing a realm in which to play out their illusion. God, however, is never forced to create the material realm by any force outside of His own will alone. It is God's merciful will that there be a realm of illusion where those particular *atmans* who have fallen under the spell of false identity (*ahamkara*) can explore their artificial sense of self, and eventually realize their true nature as eternal servants of the Divine. God is never determined, conditioned, or in any other manner constrained by any factor outside of His supremely free will.

"The essential nature of the Supreme Lord, though differentiated by space, does not undergo any change of characteristics, because He simultaneously exists everywhere." (*Brahma Sutras*, 3.2.11)

"Ishvara, the Lord, is a Purusha (Self) that has never been touched by sufferings, actions, rewards, or consequent dispositions." (*Yoga Sutras*, 1.24)

"Those devoid of reason think of Me, the unmanifest, as having manifestation, knowing not My supreme nature, imperishable, most excellent." (*Bhagavad Gita*, 7.24)

> Contemplation: Envision Sriman Narayana, the ever-free Lord of all reality. It is from the abundance of His grace alone that He wills that all reality becomes manifest.

5.5.7 Rejection of Pantheism[15]

Pantheism is the incorrect notion that the totality of every aspect of creation added together equals God. In other words, if we add up everything that exists within the material world, the end result is "God". Sometimes this mistaken idea is stated as "nature is God", or "the Cosmos is God". This false notion would make God inferior and dependent upon the creation, among the many other problems with this idea. Pantheism is the idea of God via accession rather than via supreme sovereignty. Vedic philosophy thoroughly rejects pantheism. Sanatana Dharma, rather,

---

[15] Not to be confused with pan*en*theism.

teaches the principle of panentheism, which states that God is both exceedingly transcendent in relation to His creation, while simultaneously being present imminently within it as its source and sustainer. God is within all things, but is not sourced from anything that lay outside of His own essential nature.

"Know that all opulent, beautiful and glorious creations spring from but a spark of My splendour. But what need is there, Arjuna, for all this detailed knowledge? With a single fragment of Myself I pervade and support this entire universe." (*Bhagavad Gita*, 10:41-42)

"This perceivable world is identified with the Supreme because the Supreme Brahman is the ultimate foundation of all existence, remaining unchanged as all created things are generated from it and at last dissolved into it, just as clay remains unchanged by the products made from it and again merged with it. Thus it is toward You alone that the Vedic sages direct all their thoughts, words and acts. After all, how can the footsteps of men fail to touch the earth on which they live?" (*Srimad Bhagavatam*, 10.87.15)

"As the spider moves along the thread it produces, or as from a fire tiny sparks fly in all directions, even so from this consciousness come forth all organs, all worlds, all gods, all beings. Its secret name is 'the Truth of truth.' The vital breaths are the truth and their truth is consciousness." (*Brihadaranyaka Upanishad*, 2.1.20)

"The Supreme Godhead is Himself this cosmos, and still He is aloof from it. From Him only has this cosmic manifestation emanated, in Him it rests, and unto Him it enters after annihilation." (*Srimad Bhagavatam*, 1.5.20)

"Before the creation of this cosmic manifestation, I alone existed with My specific spiritual potencies. Consciousness was then unmanifested, just as one's consciousness is unmanifested during the time of sleep. I am the reservoir of unlimited potency, and therefore I am known as unlimited or all-pervading. From My material energy the cosmic manifestation appeared within Me, and in this universal manifestation appeared the chief being, Lord Brahma, who is not born of a material mother and is your source." (*Srimad Bhagavatam*, 6.4.47-48)

> Exercise: Take a hike deep into nature, either alone or with people you love. Breathe in the beauty and harmony of all you see around you in the grandeur of nature. Know that Brahman is the source of all you are experiencing around you, and that it is His very presence within all of nature that gives nature her beauty and healing power.

5.5.8 Brahman as the Source

In the next two sections (5.5.8 and 5.5.9), we examine the relationship of Brahman (God) and the creation (Jagat) in connection with the four Aristotelian Causes: that is, the material, formal, efficient and final causes.

Creation does not proceed from nothing (*ex nihilo*), as is the claim of the Abrahamic religions. Rather, God is both the Material Cause and the Efficient Cause of creation. God is the Material Cause in that the very building blocks of all material objects are transformations of His material energy (*prakriti*). God is the Efficient Cause in that He is the agent through whose will creation eventually comes about.

Aum purnam adah purnam idam
purnat purnam udachyate
purnasya purnam adaya
purnam evavashishyate

"That Absolute is perfect and complete, and because He is completely perfect, all emanations from Him, such as this phenomenal world, are perfectly equipped as complete wholes. Whatever is produced of the

Complete Whole is also complete in itself. Because He is the Complete Whole, even though so many complete units emanate from Him, He remains the complete balance." (*Isha Upanishad*, Invocation)

"As the spider sends forth and draws in its thread, as plants grow on the earth, as hair grows on the head and the body of a living person - so does everything in the universe arise from the Imperishable." (*Mundaka Upanishad*, 1.1.7)

"The Supreme Godhead, the original person, has multifarious energies. He is the origin of material creation, and it is due to Him only that everything changes. He is the protector of Dharma and annihilator of all sinful activities. He is the master of all opulences." (*Shvetashvatara Upanishad*, 6.6)

Question: What does not have God as its source?

Contemplation: As we observe the world around us, let us think about the amazing fact that every good thing that is perceivable and conceivable to us has God as its source.

5.5.9 The Final Goal and the Final Cause

As the ultimate source of Dharma, which constitutes the ordering principles of the cosmos, Brahman is the Formal Cause of Jagat (materiality). Brahman, via Dharma, is the archetypal model of cosmic order. More, He is also the Final cause in that the material universe has its ultimate repose in Him as one of His energies. Every individual *atman*, too, has Brahman as his or her Final Cause in that it is their ultimate destiny to eventually be united with Him again. God is the final goal of all things. God is the final meaning of all things.

"Gold alone is present before its manufacture into gold products, the gold alone remains after the products' destruction, and the gold alone is the essential reality while it is being utilized under various designations. Similarly, I alone exist before the creation of this universe, after its destruction and during its maintenance." (Sri Krishna, *Srimad Bhagavatam*, 11.28.19)

"He is the Lord of all. He is the knower of all. He is the inner controller. He is the source of all; for from Him all beings originate and in Him they finally disappear." (*Mandukya Upanishad*, 1.6)

"He who knows Brahman, which is the cause, not an effect, which is conscious, which is without end, as hidden in the cave of the heart, in the highest ether, he enjoys all blessings, at one with the omniscient Brahman." (*Taittiriya Upanishad*, 2.1.2)

Questions: What personal goals do you have in your life? How can you link your goals with the ultimate goal of knowing God?

5.5.10 Proving God's Existence

It is disingenuous of the atheist to demand sensory "proof" for God's existence. This is the case because God transcends materiality. Thus, the material senses are insufficient for "proving" God's existence. It is similar to demanding empirical, or sensory, proof that a human person possesses a mind. There is no empirical proof for the existence of any individual's mind, including that of the atheist. Rather, we know that a person has a mind because we can infer its existence due to observing the characteristics of a mind, but not by seeing, hearing or smelling a mind. It is a process of reasoning contained in our mind itself that reveals the existence of other people's minds to us!

In addition, merely having intellectual proof of God's existence is insufficient spiritually, since the mere intellectual acknowledgement of God's existence is insufficient to ensure that a person will then desire to know God fully, or to pursue a meaningful spiritual life. How many people are there who claim to believe in God, but who actually have no desire to either know Him or to serve His divine will? Thus, the best "proof" of God's existence is a radically experiential and personal one. It is through our own consciousness that we can know that Supreme Consciousness.

"Brahman (God) is not grasped by the eye, nor by speech, nor by the other senses, nor by penance or good works. A person becomes pure through serenity of intellect; thereupon, in meditation, he beholds Him who is without parts." (*Mundaka Upanishad*, 3.1.8)

> Questions: What personal experiential evidences have you had of God's reality? If none, how can you change that? If you have had some, how can you increase those experiences?
>
> If God's existence were intellectually proven to you without any doubt, what would you then do with that knowledge?

5.6.1 C) The Material Cosmos

Section C of chapter five focuses on the nature of Jagat, or materiality and the material world. It examines several aspects of cosmology and cosmogony.

Vedic Cosmology: The Tripartite Universe and Multiverses

Each material universe is composed of a hierarchy of three realms. From the lowest to the highest, these three planes are:

A) Hellish Plane

B) Earthly Plane

C) Heavenly Plane

The lowest realm is the Hellish plane. Many demonic beings (*asuras*) make their home there. The cultures and civilizations of the Hellish realms are very diverse. Some are even very technologically advanced. But their technology is used for evil and conquest.

Above the Hellish domain, there is the Earthly plane. This middle area is the realm of humans (*manushya*) and human-like beings. In addition to the particular Earth planet that we inhabit, there are many similar planets inhabited by human beings. There are 400,000 different species, or races, of humans. A few of the human races that occupy other planets are much more physically, technologically and spiritually advanced than we are. But they are still technically human.

Finally, there is what is commonly called the Heavenly plane, which is not to be confused with the eternal spiritual realm, which transcends all three realms within the material universes.[16] The Heavenly plane is a sector of our material universe that is the home of various strata of gods (*devas*) and goddesses (*devis*), who are beneficent beings of light who serve

---

[16] This confusion often arises because the Abrahamic religions also call their god's kingdom "Heaven" in the English language.

God in the functioning of the material universe. The actual spiritual realm (Vaikuntha) is vastly beyond the Heavenly realm.

The Vedic scriptures also teach us that our universe is not the only material universe in existence. Rather, there are an almost unlimited number of universes of varying sizes within the entirety of the material realm. Each universe has a similar tripartite structure as ours does, with Hellish, Earthly and Heavenly realms.

God's superior spiritual energy is known as Para-prakriti. His marginal energy, which consists of all *atmans*, is known as Tatashta-shakti. Finally, His material energy is Apara-prakriti. It is from the Apara-prakriti that the material universes all unfold.

"The Supreme Lord has nothing to do, and no one is found to be equal to or greater than Him, for everything is done naturally and systematically by His multifarious energies." (*Shvetashvatara Upanishad*, 6.8)

"The residents of both heaven and hell desire human birth on the earth planet because human life facilitates the achievement of transcendental knowledge and love of Godhead, whereas neither heavenly nor hellish bodies efficiently provide such opportunities." (*Uddhava Gita*, 15:12)

"I am never manifest to the foolish and unintelligent. For them I am covered by My internal potency, and therefore they do not know that I am unborn and infallible." (Sri Krishna, *Bhagavad Gita*, 7:25)

"Living in the abyss of ignorance, the deluded think themselves blest. Attached to works, they know not God. Works lead them only to the heavenly realm, whence, to their sorrow, their rewards quickly exhausted, they are flung back to earth. Considering religion to be observance of rituals and performance of acts of charity, the deluded remain ignorant of the highest good. Having enjoyed in the heavenly realms the reward of their good works, they enter again into the world of mortals." (*Mundaka*

Upanishad, 1:2:9-10)

"Even the entirety of whatever there may be within the three worlds to satisfy one's senses cannot satisfy a person whose senses are uncontrolled." (*Srimad Bhagavatam*, 8.19.21)

Fact: We can reincarnate, in accordance with our *karma*, in any of the three realms (Hellish, Earthly or Heavenly), or even in another universe. Wherever we find ourselves living within the material universe, however, that is only a temporary home until our *karma* runs out and we then need to reincarnate again. The only liberation from this cycle of reincarnation is to fully transcend the material world altogether. We accomplish such transcendence by following the eternal path of the *rishis*, the ancient seer-sages and perfected yogis who revealed the Vedic scriptures to us.

Exercise: By meditating upon the Gayatri *mantra*, we have the ability to traverse systematically through the higher realms until we eventually experience the very light of God. Meditate upon the Gayatri *mantra* each day.[17]

Aum Bhur Bhuvah Svaha
Tat Savitur Varenyam
Bhargo Devasya Dhimahi
Dhiyo Yo Naha Prachodayat Aum

---

[17] This famous *mantra* is found in *Rig Veda*, 3.62.10. The translation is: "I invoke the Earth Plane, the Astral Plane, the Plane of Intellect, and the Plane of Absolute Truth. The resplendent effulgence and divine brilliance of God is pure and venerable. We pray and meditate on God to inspire our minds and illuminate our intellect with His divine light."

5.6.2 The Three Gunas: The Metaphysical Grounding of Physical Reality

Materiality in the most general of senses is known variously as *prakriti*, *pradhana* or Jagat. Everything and anything that is not purely spiritual, or purely consciousness, is by default material. Material things include not only the obvious (insentient matter and our bodies, for example), but also our material emotions, minds, intellect and false sense of self (*ahamkara*). All of these are temporary, restricted, deficient, and thus material.

While materiality can become temporarily assembled to form any of the many objects that we see around us, when it is broken down to its essential form, materiality is ultimately an energy. It is one of God's many diverse energies and powers. That material energy, when further analyzed, can be seen as existing on three different frequencies.

These frequencies are the three *gunas*, or modes of material energy. The three *gunas* are:

A) *Sattva* (goodness, purity, light, healthfulness, wholeness)

B) *Rajas* (passion, energetic, creativity, productivity)

C) *Tamas* (dullness, lethargy, ignorance, impurity, darkness)

Anything that is material has all of these three *gunas* within it, but with one of them being predominant. For human beings, our goal is to cultivate pure *sattva* in our hearts, minds and bodies. The best way to achieve this is to only allow sattvic things to enter our senses, since what enters our senses creates who we are.

"Deluded by the three *gunas*, the whole world does not know Me who am above the *gunas* and inexhaustible. This divine energy of Mine, consisting of the three *gunas* of material nature, is difficult to overcome. But those who have surrendered unto Me can easily cross beyond it." (*Bhagavad Gita*, 7.13-14)

"Those who strongly desire to cross the ocean of nescience must not associate with the modes of ignorance (*tamas*), for hedonistic activities are the greatest obstructions to realization of Dharma, economic development (*artha*), fulfillment of desire (*kama*) and, at last, liberation (*moksha*)." (*Srimad Bhagavatam*, 4.22.34)

Questions: What are some foods that are sattvic, rajasic and ta-masic? What are some forms of entertainment, behavior and practices that fall into these three categories?

Exercise: In the book *Sanatana Dharma: The Eternal Natural Way*, we have provided some important guidelines to leading a sattvic life. Below is an expansion of those guidelines that you should begin practicing in order to avoid the lower *gunas*. These are some of the practices you should adopt to live a sattvic lifestyle:

The Sattvic Program

1) Practice Yoga on a regular basis. This includes both the physical exercises known as *asanas*, and the other limbs of Ashtanga Yoga (the Yoga of Eight Limbs).

2) Observe a purely vegetarian diet that emphasizes healthy, natural and organic foods. Avoid processed foods, fast foods, foods cooked by strangers and genetically modified foods as much as possible.

3) Rid your mind of all negative, violent, sexually explicit and disturbing thoughts and images. This includes horror movies, the propaganda of mainstream media, images of skulls and dark deities, and all pornography.

96

4) Avoid all entertainment and music that is charged with explicitly sexual (tamasic) or violent (rajasic) lyrics, such as "rap", "black metal", "death metal" and "hip-hop" music and lifestyles.

5) Meditate daily on the *mantra* **Aum Namo Narayanaya** with great dedication and devotion.

6) Associate with other people who are also leading a sattvic lifestyle. Learn from such people. Absorb their positive energy. Grow in their good company. Conversely, completely avoid the company of any and all negative, morally corrupt and manipulative people. Seek always the company of the good.

7) As much as possible, place yourself in the beauty of nature. Take hikes, meditate, breathe in deeply, and contemplate in deep natural surroundings. Visit beautiful gardens as much as possible.

8) Always try to lovingly commune with the gods (*devas*), goddesses (*devis*), positive nature spirits (Yakshas), and other beneficent beings who represent light and goodness. Always avoid worshipping and communing with any metaphysical beings who are inherently dark and evil in any way. Only evil people worship such beings. Also avoid the company of people who ignorantly commune with such dark and evil deities. We become like that upon which we meditate. Our goal is to become beings of light, wisdom and goodness, not the opposite.

Chapter 6 Ethics: Walking the Talk

The observance of an ethical lifestyle is central to what it means to be a serious follower of Sanatana Dharma. We do not believe that ethical principles are relative or subjective, but that God Himself reveals such principles to us through the Vedic scriptures and through the examples of all the great sages. It is in Vedic ethics that we put the philosophy of Sanatana Dharma into actual practice in our relationship with others.

Chapter six focuses on several different aspects of Vedic ethics.

"Those who are demonic do not know what is to be done and what is not to be done. Neither cleanliness, nor proper behavior, nor truth is found in them." (*Bhagavad Gita*, 16.7)

6.1.1 The Virtue-Ethics System of Sanatana Dharma

There are two forms of ethics: Proscriptive Ethics and Virtue Ethics. With Proscriptive Ethics, ethical behavior is enforced from external sources in the form of rules and regulations. In Virtue Ethics, ethical behavior is cultivated internally as a process of the natural unfolding of the inherent goodness of our soul. Sanatana Dharma follows the Virtue Ethics model more so than the Proscriptive Ethics model.

The goal of every Dharmi is to personify the Good in our lives. This means incorporating the Good in everything we do by living an ethical lifestyle. There are two forms of goodness: a) good as a virtue, and b) good in action. It is the inherent virtue of the *atman* to be good. The Dharmi cultivates goodness as a natural virtue by practicing goodness in action. We do this by cultivating goodness in everything that we think, say and do. We derive our knowledge of what is ethical and unethical behavior from the teachings of the Vedic scriptures.

samah shatrau cha mitre cha tatha manapamanayoh
shitoshna-sukha-duhkheshu samah sanga-vivarjitah

tulya-ninda-stutir mauni santushto yena kenachit
aniketah sthira-matir bhaktiman me priyo narah

98

"One who is equal to friends and enemies, who is equipoised in honor and dishonor, heat and cold, happiness and distress, fame and infamy, who is always free from contamination, always silent and satisfied with anything, who doesn't care for any residence, who is fixed in knowledge and engaged in devotional service, is very dear to Me." (*Bhagavad Gita*, 12.18-19)

*amanitvam adambhitvam ahimsa kshantir arjavam
acharyopasanam shaucam sthairyam atma-vinigrahah*

*indriyartheshu vairagyam anahankara eva cha
janma-mrtyu-jara-vyadhi duhkha-doshanudarshanam*

*ashaktir anabhishvangah putra-dara-grhadishu
nityam cha sama-chittatvam ishtanishtopapattishu*

*mayi chananya-yogena bhaktir avyabhicharini
vivikta-desha-sevitvam aratir jana-samsadi*

*adhyatma-jnana-nityatvam tattva-jnanartha-darshanam
etaj jnanam iti proktam ajnanam yad ato 'nyatha*

"Humility, pridelessness, nonviolence, tolerance, simplicity, approaching a true spiritual master, cleanliness, steadiness and self-control; renunciation of the objects of sense gratification, absence of false ego, the perception of the evil of birth, death, old age and disease; nonattachment to children, wife, home and the rest, and even-mindedness amid pleasant and unpleasant events; constant and unalloyed devotion to Me, resorting to solitary places, detachment from the general mass of people; accepting the importance of self-realization, and philosophical search for the Absolute Truth - all these I thus declare to be knowledge, and what is contrary to these is ignorance." (*Bhagavad Gita*, 13.8-12)

"He who has found the bliss of the Eternal is afflicted no more by the thought, 'Why have I not done the good? Why have I done evil?' One who knows the self extricates himself from both these things." (*Taittiriya Upanishad*, 2.9)

"O My sons, you should accept a highly elevated *paramahamsa*, a spiritually advanced spiritual master. In this way, you should place your faith and love in Me, the Supreme Godhead. You should reject sense gratification and tolerate the duality of pleasure and pain, which are like the seasonal changes of summer and winter. Try to realize the miserable condition of living entities, who are miserable even in the higher planetary systems. Philosophically inquire about the truth. Then undergo all kinds of austerities and penances for the sake of devotional service. Give up the endeavor for sense enjoyment and engage in the service of the Lord. Listen to discussions about the Supreme Godhead, and always associate with devotees. Chant about and glorify the Supreme Lord, and look upon everyone equally on the spiritual platform. Give up enmity and subdue anger and lamentation. Abandon identifying the self with the body and the home, and practice reading the revealed scriptures. Live in a secluded place and practice the process by which you can completely control your life air, mind and senses. Have full faith in the revealed scriptures, the Vedic literatures, and always observe celibacy. Perform your prescribed duties and avoid unnecessary talks. Always thinking of the Supreme Godhead, acquire knowledge from the right source. Thus practicing Yoga, you will patiently and enthusiastically be elevated in knowledge and will be able to give up the false ego." (Rishabha, the "founder" of Jainism, teaching his sons; *Srimad Bhagavatam*, 5.5.10-13)

> Exercise: Using the above verses from the scriptures as a perfect guide, honestly assess the inner virtues that you know you need to work on. Having done silent breath concentration for a few minutes, know that such virtues are an inherent part of your true self. Such virtues arise from your *atman*, or true self. Visualize what it would look like to practice one or more of these virtues in your daily life. Finally, practice these virtues each day until they become second nature to you.

6.1.2 Ten Ethical Principles of Dharma

While there are many ethical principles that are revealed in the Vedic scriptures, as seen from the scriptural examples above, there are ten specific principles that are seen as the bare minimum requirement that each Dharmi must follow. These ten ethical principles are known as the

100

Yamas and Niyamas. These are found in the Yoga system, but they are an inherent part of the Sanatana Dharma tradition as a whole.

"A wise person should observe both prohibitory (*yama*) as well as positive (*niyama*) injunctions. A person who fails to conform to these becomes a debased person." (*Manava Dharma Shastra*, 4.204)

Five Yamas - Proscriptions

These are five behaviors that will help us avoid unethical actions.

• **Ahimsa** (non-violence)

"*Ahimsa* is not causing pain to any living being at any time through the actions of one's mind, speech or body." (*Shandilya Upanishad*, 1.1)

"When one is confirmed in non-violence, hostility ceases in his presence." (*Yoga Sutras*, 2.35)

• **Satya** (truthfulness)

satyam eva jayate nanrtam
satyena pantha vitato devayanah
yenakramantyrsayo hyaptakama
yatra tat satyasya paramam nidhanam

"Truth alone triumphs; not falsehood. Through truth the divine path is spread out by which the sages whose desires have been completely fulfilled, reach where that supreme treasure of Truth resides." (*Mundaka Upanishad*, 3.1.6)

"When one is firmly established in truth, the fruits of action become subservient to him." (*Yoga Sutras*, 2.36)

• **Asteya** (non-stealing)

"All jewels approach him who is confirmed in honesty and non-stealing." (*Yoga Sutras*, 2.37)

• **Brahmacharya** (sexual continence)

"When one is confirmed in sexual control, spiritual vigor is gained." (*Yoga Sutras*, 2.38)

"The *brahmachari* (one who observes *brahmacharya*) moves, strengthening both the worlds, in him the *devas* meet in concord; he upholds Earth and Heaven; he satisfies his Acharya with the power of austerity." (*Atharva Veda*, 11.5.1)

• **Aparigraha** (non-possessiveness)

"When one is confirmed in non-possessiveness, the knowledge of the why and how of existence is attained." (*Yoga Sutras*, 2.39)

Niyamas - Prescriptions

These are five behaviors to be cultivated.

• **Shaucha** (purity)

"From purity follows a withdrawal from enchantment over one's own body as well as a cessation of desire for physical contact with others."(*Yoga Sutras*, 2.40)

• **Santosha** (contentment)

yam hi na vyathayanty ete purusham purusharsabha
sama-duhkha-sukham dhiram so 'mrtatvaya kalpate

"O best among men [Arjuna], the person who is not disturbed by happiness and distress and is steady in both is certainly eligible for liberation." (*Bhagavad Gita*, 2.15)

"As a result of contentment there is purity of mind, one-pointedness, control of the senses, and fitness for the vision of the self. Supreme happiness is gained via contentment. " (*Yoga Sutras*, 2.41-42)

• **Tapas** (austerity)

"Through austerity and the removal of impurities, there arise special powers in the body and senses." (*Yoga Sutras*, 2.43)

• **Svadhyaya** (self-education)

"By study comes communion with the Lord in the desired Form. (Yoga Sutras, 2.44)

• **Ishvara-Pranidhana** (devotion to the Divine)

"From a special process of dedicated devotion to God (*ishvara-pranidhana*), the coming of *samadhi* (spiritual absorption) is imminent." (*Yoga Sutras*, 1.23)

"By total surrender to God, *samadhi* is attained." (*Yoga Sutras*, 2.45)

<u>Contemplation</u>: All ten of these principles are not merely an arbitrary set of rules that are imposed upon us from some external source. Rather, they are virtues that naturally arise from our eternal spiritual identity.

<u>Questions</u>: How can I increase *ahimsa* in my daily life?

Does *satya*, or truthfulness, mean simply always telling the truth, or also living in Truth?

Does *brahmacharya* mean I need to be a celibate monk to be a successful *yogi*? What if I am married?

How can we say that *santosha* is a virtue?

What are some practical examples of *tapas* (austerity)?

How is *ishvara-pranidhana* the most important of these ten principles?

This section also mentions twelve qualities that followers of Sanatana Dharma should try to cultivate in themselves. These qualities are:

1. Humility

2. Simplicity

3. Devotion

4. Compassion

5. Loyalty

6. Wisdom

7. Equanimity

8. Balance

9. Excellence

10. Discernment

11. Strength

12. Courage

"In my right hand is the effort, and the success is in my left hand."

(*Atharva Veda*, 7.50.8)

> Contemplation: Like the Yamas and Niyamas, these twelve quali-
> ties are innate characteristics of our very soul. They are to be
> cultivated from within.

6.2.1 A Comparative Analysis of Dharmic Ethics and the Judeo-Christian Ten Commandments

In this section of the book (6.2.1-6.2.8), we do a comparative analysis of
the Vedic view of ethics versus the Abrahamic view by contrasting the
ten principles of Yama-Niyama against the Ten Commandments.

6.2.2 Diversity of Ethical Systems

There are many different ethical and moral codes to be found in the diverse religions and cultures of this world. While there is certainly some
overlap between these varying systems, it would be dishonest to say that
all religions share the exact same moral code. For many of the Abrahamic
religions, for example, it was historically considered to be virtuous to
persecute and even kill followers of non-Abrahamic religions. For the
Dharmic religions, on the other hand, to kill another person merely because they follow a different religion would be considered highly
immoral. The ethical system of Sanatana Dharma is based upon the principle of compassion toward all beings.

"One should never do that to another which one regards as injurious to
one's own self. This, in brief, is the rule of *dharma*. Yielding to desire and
acting differently from this principle, one becomes guilty of *adharma* (an-

ti-Dharma)." (*Mahabharata*, 18.113.8)

"Let us have concord with our own people, and concord with people who are strangers to us; Ashvins, create between us and the strangers a unity of hearts. May we unite in our midst, unite in our purposes, and not fight against the divine spirit within us. Let not the battle-cry rise amidst many slain, nor the arrows of the War-God fall with the break of day." (*Atharva Veda*, 15.7.52)

"May all beings look at me with a friendly eye. May I do likewise, and may we all look on each other with the eyes of a friend." (*Yajur Veda*, 36.18)

> Fact: The ethical principles of Sanatana Dharma are not based upon blind faith, subjective opinions, dogmas or taboos. They are based upon the realization of those personal qualities that most ably lead to virtuous and noble thoughts, words and actions on the part of the person; as well as the avoidance of those misconducts that lead to inimical thoughts, words and actions. Ethics is more of an art than a science, but it is an art that is revealed in impeccable sublimity by the Vedic scriptures.

6.2.3 Differences between Dharmic and Judeo-Christian world-views

As alluded to above, the Dharmic and Abrahamic world-views are radically different from one another, and in some instances, diametrically opposed to one another. One of the philosophical differences between Dharma and Abrahamism is in their respective views on the nature of the human person. For Dharma, the human person is understood to be primarily an eternal soul (*atman*), who temporarily inhabits a physical body. For Abrahamism, on the other hand, the human person is a matrix of soul and body. There cannot be a human person if one of these two elements is missing.

Another distinction between these two world-views involves the locus of, and motivation for, ethical behavior. For Dharma, virtue is an internal concern of the individual person, and ethical behavior is motivated by a desire to exceed spiritually. For Abrahamism, morality is an exterior-based communal concern, and is motivated by fear of transgression against, and subsequent punishment from, the Abrahamic deity.

"For the soul there is neither birth nor death at any time. He has not come into being, does not come into being, and will not come into being. He is unborn, eternal, ever-existing and primeval. He is not slain when the body is slain." (*Bhagavad Gita*, 2.20)

"'He therefore that knows it, after having become quiet, subdued, satisfied, patient, and collected, sees his self in the Absolute, sees all as dependent upon the Absolute. Evil does not overcome him, he overcomes all evil. Evil does not burn him, he burns all evil. Free from evil, free from spots, free from doubts, he becomes a (true) *brahmana*; this is the Brahma-world, O King,' thus spoke Yajñavalkya." (*Brihadaranyaka Upanishad*, 4:4.23.)

> Fact: The Dharmi is not motivated to be a virtuous and ethical person due to fear. The Dharmi is virtuous because he is consciously cultivating the enhancement of an inherent characteristic of his soul, and he is ethical due to compassion for other living beings.

6.2.4 Inherent Virtue Ethics and Proscribed Ethics

Dharma follows the Virtue Ethics model. Dharmic ethics is predicated upon the knowledge that virtue is an inherent trait of the soul that needs to be cultivated and brought to the surface. The soul is already perfect since it is a reflection of the Supreme Perfect. We have only forgotten this fact, and need to remember it. Abrahamism follows the Proscribed Ethics model. For Abrahamism, ethics consists of a set of dogmatic rules that are imposed upon the person from external sources.

"Now follow the eight good inherent qualities of the soul. Compassion on all creatures, forbearance, freedom from anger, purity, quietism, auspiciousness, freedom from avarice, and freedom from covetousness. He who is sanctified by the forty sacraments, but whose soul is destitute of these eight good qualities, will not be united with Brahman, nor does he reach His abode. But he who is sanctified by a few only of the forty sacraments, and whose soul is endowed with these eight excellent qualities, will be united with Brahman, and will dwell in His abode." (*Gautama Dharma Sutra*, 8:22)

"Some look on the soul as amazing, some describe him as amazing, and some hear of him as amazing, while others, even after hearing about him, cannot understand him at all." (*Bhagavad Gita*, 2.29)

> Guidance: Vedic spirituality teaches that the soul (*atman*) is inherently good. At present, of course, that inherent goodness is temporarily covered up and sometimes inaccessible to us due to our current state of illusion (*maya*). It is for this reason that the goal of ethics in Sanatana Dharma is more of a reclaiming of our original state of goodness, than an attempt to artificially impose goodness from outside of ourselves. This is in stark contrast to the Christian notion of Original Sin, in which the human person is seen as being inherently fallen and sinful. We reject this short-sighted dogma entirely.

6.2.5 Shruti Versus Smriti

From a scriptural epistemology perspective, Abrahamism views the laws of morality as having been revealed by their deity within the context of temporal history. Thus, the Ten Commandments, for example, were first revealed during the lifetime of Moses, sometime around 1400 to 1500 B.C.E. For Sanatana Dharma, on the other hand, the scriptural source of principles of virtue is based upon eternal Truth. True ethical principles cannot be historically bound, but must be eternal by nature.

"The *Veda* is the eternal eyesight for ancestors, gods, and humans; for Vedic teaching is beyond the powers of logic or cognition." (*Manava Dharma Shastra*, 12.94)

> Fact: The technical term for the knowledge that is revealed in the Vedic scriptures is *apaurusheya*, which means "non-manmade". Vedic knowledge does not simply arise somewhere within the context of material history as a result of some person's speculation or intellectual creativity. Rather, Vedic knowledge has always eternally existed. It is accessed, and then revealed to humanity, by perfected *yogis* known as *rishis* (seer-sages).

6.2.6 Ten Principles of Yoga

The Ten Principles are again explained here in order to compare them specifically with the Ten Commandments of the Bible.

"Under *yama* are ten: *ahimsa, satya, asteya, brahmacharya, daya, arjava, kshama, dhriti, mitahara* and *saucha*. Of these, *ahimsa* is the not causing of any pain to any living being at any time through the actions of one's mind, speech, or body. *Satya* is the speaking of the truth that conduces to the well-being of creatures, through the actions of one's mind, speech, or body. *Asteya* is not coveting of another's property through the actions of one's mind, speech, or body. *Brahmacharya* is the refraining from inappropriate sexual conduct in all places and in all states in mind, speech or body. *Daya* is kindliness towards all creatures in all places. *Arjava* is the preserving of equanimity of mind, speech, or body in the performance or non-performance of the actions ordained or forbidden to be done. *Kshama* is the bearing patiently of all pleasant or unpleasant things, such as praise or blow. *Dhriti* is the preserving of firmness of mind during the period of gain or loss of wealth or relatives. *Mitahara* is the taking of oily and sweet food, leaving one-fourth of the stomach empty. *Shaucha* is of two kinds, external and internal. Of these, the external is the cleansing of the body by earth and water; the internal is the cleansing of the mind. This (the latter) is to be obtained by means of the *adhyatma-vidya* (Science of Self)." (*Shandilya Upanishad*, 1.1)

"Under *niyama* are ten: *tapas, santosha astikya, dana, ishvarapujana, siddhanta-shravana, hrih, mati, japa* and *vrata*. Of these *tapas*, is the emancipation of the body through the observances of such penances as *krichchhra, chandra-yana*, etc., according to rules. *Santosha* is being satisfied with whatever comes to us of its own accord. *Astikya* is the belief in the merits or de-merits of actions as stated in the *Vedas*. *Dana* is the giving with faith to deserving persons, money, grains, etc., earned lawfully. *Ishvarapujana* is the worshipping of Vishnu with pure mind according to one's power. *Sid-dhanta-Shravana* is the inquiry into the significance of Vedanta. *Hrih* is the remorse felt in the performance of things contrary to the rules of the *Vedas* and of society. *Mati* is the faith in the paths laid down by the *Ve-das*. *Japa* is the practising of the *mantras* into which one is duly initiated by his spiritual instructor and which is not against (the rules of) the *Vedas*. It is of two kinds - the spoken and the mental. The mental is associated with contemplation by the mind. The spoken is of two kinds – the loud and the low. The loud pronunciation gives the reward as stated (in the *Vedas*): (while) the low one gives a reward a thousand times that. The mental gives a reward of one-hundred thousand times that. *Vrata* is the regular observance of or the refraining from the actions enjoined or pro-hibited by the *Vedas*." (*Shandilya Upanishad*, 1.2)

Exercise: If you wish to fully experience the goal of the path of Yoga, then strive to put the principles mentioned above in the

Shandilya Upanishad into daily practice in your life.

6.2.7 Comparative Analysis of the Ten Commandments and the Ten Principles

In this comparison of the Ten Commandments and the Ten Principles, it is shown that the former are externally oriented laws that are imposed upon the worshiper. The Ten Principles, on the other hand, are principles of internal virtuous growth that the spiritual practitioner is meant to cultivate within himself as a manifestation of his inherent spiritual goodness. Such virtues are known via the Vedic scriptures, and by observing the behavior of noble sages. It is in emulating the behavior of noble beings that we cultivate proper behavior in ourselves. Despite some minimal overlap, these two sets of moral guidelines are very different from each other, with each pertaining specifically to the tradition in which they were born.

"The righteous and the unrighteous do not go around saying, 'Here we are!' Nor do the gods, Gandharvas, or ancestors declare, 'This is righteous and that is unrighteous.' An activity that the Noble Ones (*aryas*) praise is righteous, and what they deplore is unrighteous. He should model his conduct after that which is unanimously approved in all regions by the Noble Ones (*aryas*) who have been properly trained, who are elderly and self-possessed, and who are neither greedy nor deceitful. In this way, he will win both worlds." (*Apastamba Dharma Sutras*, 1.20)

Question: What are some examples of noble people whom you have learned from and emulated?

Guidance: Nobility is encouraged in Vedic culture, not in the class sense, but in the sense of magnanimous personal behavior.

A person is noble, not by birth, but by their temperament and actions. The definition of nobility (*aryatva*) is the following. A noble person (*arya*) acts from a place of benevolence, and never malice; seeks excellence in everything he does and in his environment; very conscientiously observes all principles of chivalry and etiquette; never lacks the courage and inner strength to stand up for truth and justice; always finds his inspiration in higher sources, and never merely in public opinion or his own baser needs.

6.2.8 Decalogue and Dialog

Religions are all different. While recognizing these differences, however, it is important to ensure the freedom of individuals to practice the religion of their choice.

ekam sad vipra bahudha vadanti

"Truth is One, despite sages calling it by various names." (*Rig Veda*, 1.164.46)

6.3.1 The Twelve Qualities of a Dharmi

In this section, we revisit the twelve qualities that every follower of Sanatana Dharma should try to develop. These are twelve inner virtues, or qualities, that all superior human beings should cultivate within themselves.

1. Humility

2. Simplicity

3. Devotion

4. Compassion

5. Loyalty

6. Wisdom

7. Equanimity

8. Balance

9. Excellence

10. Discernment

11. Strength

12. Courage

"When a person completely gives up all the culpable desires he is harboring in his heart, he exchanges mortality for eternal spiritual life and attains real pleasure in the Absolute Truth." (*Brhad-Aranyaka Upanishad*, 4.4.9)

> Questions: Which of these qualities do I already see within myself? Which of these qualities do I especially need to work on? How can I increase this quality within me?

6.4.1 The Four Jewels (Chatur Ratna)

There are several prerequisites that are necessary for anyone who is beginning the spiritual path, and to continue to deepen as we progress further along the path. The most important of these behavioral principles are what are called the Four Jewels.

Humility (*dainya*)

Simplicity (*saralata*)

Devotion (*bhakti*)

Compassion (*karuna*)

1) Humility means understanding and accepting one's natural place in the universe, and not allowing false ego to determine one's course of action.

2) Simplicity means being satisfied with what is minimally necessary in life in order to pursue the spiritual path with health and free from all material anxiety.

3) Devotion means practicing the path with love toward God and *guru*.

4) Compassion means sharing the teachings of Dharma with others to the best of our capacity. When we live these Four Jewels, our spiritual life becomes rich and sweet.

> Exercise: To cultivate humility, visualize yourself serving Krishna with great devotion each day in meditation. To exercise more simplicity, honestly assess your life to see what extravagances you can reduce. Increase your devotion toward God and *guru* by consciously thinking loving thoughts about them throughout the day. Express compassion by sharing the teachings of Sanatana Dharma with others to the best of your ability.

6.5.1 Honoring Life: The Principles of Vegetarianism

One of the most important of the Ten Principles of Sanatana Dharma is *ahimsa*, or non-violence. The most crucial way that we practice *ahimsa* is by following a vegetarian diet. Though a small handful of atheist philosophers and Abrahamic theologians have attempted to offer pseudo-philosophical arguments for why there are no moral implications to following a non-vegetarian diet, these arguments all ultimately fail because they confuse a) a moral agent with b) an object of moral concern. A living being does not have to be a moral agent in order to be an object of moral concern. The criterion for being an object of moral concern is not the ability to either think rationally or to express oneself verbally, but having the ability to feel pain. If any beings experience pain, then they are objects of moral concern, and it is our moral obligation to not harm them. Eating them harms them. Therefore, it is our moral obligation to be vegetarian.

"Those noble souls who practice meditation and other yogic ways, who are ever careful about all beings, who protect all animals, are the ones who are actually serious about spiritual practices." (*Atharva Veda Samhita*, 19.48.5)

"You must not use your God-given body for killing God's creatures, whether they are human, animal or of any other kind." (*Yajur Veda Samhita*, 12.32)

"The purchaser of flesh performs violence by his wealth. He who eats flesh does so by enjoying its taste. The killer does violence by actually tying and killing the animal. Thus, there are three forms of killing: he who brings flesh or sends for it, he who cuts off the limbs of an animal, and he who purchases, sells or cooks flesh and eats it—all of these are to be considered meat-eaters." (*Mahabharata, Anuparva*, 115.40)

Questions: Why is it acceptable to eat a cow, but not to eat a dog or cat? Have you ever experienced such emotions as love or fear from your pet dog or cat? Do animals suffer?

Guidance: The goal of *ahimsa* is not absolute non-violence, because that is an impossibility. Rather, the realistic goal is to minimize violence as much as is possible. It is for this reason that we as vegetarians will not eat meat, fish or eggs, but we will eat plants. While it is true that plants also are alive, it has been shown scientifically that they feel a very minimal amount of suffering. Therefore, as vegetarians, we are eating while also causing the least amount of pain possible.

6.5.2 Vegetarianism for a Better World

There are actually many reasons for being vegetarian, in addition to the ethical reasons. Vegetarianism is a healthier diet, improves the economy, and helps the environment.

"If required, one should endeavor to get sufficient foodstuffs, because it is always necessary and proper to maintain one's health. When the senses, mind and life air are fit, one can contemplate spiritual truth, and by understanding the truth one is liberated." (*Uddhava Gita*, 13:34)

"Meat can never be obtained without injury to living creatures, and injury to sentient beings is detrimental to the attainment of heavenly bliss; let him therefore shun the use of meat. Having well considered the disgusting origin of flesh and the cruelty of fettering and slaying corporeal beings, let him entirely abstain from eating flesh." (*Manava Dharma Shastra*, 5.48-49)

"Those high-souled persons who desire beauty, faultlessness of limbs, long life, understanding, mental and physical strength and memory should abstain from acts of injury." (*Mahabharata*, 18.115.8)

Guidance: The best way to become vegetarian, if you are not vegetarian already, is to do so as a slow transition, taking between 3-6 months. Begin your transition to vegetarianism by first eliminating all red meats from your diet, especially beef. After some time, then stop eating all meats, including such "white" meats as chicken. After this, stop eating all fish. Finally, give up eggs. Dairy products, such as milk, yogurt and cheese, are completely acceptable in a Vedic vegetarian diet. We do not believe in veganism, since a vegan diet needs to be supplemented with B-vitamins. And being forced to take vitamins to supplement a diet means that it is an unnatural diet. Rather, the Vedic scriptures clearly recommend a lacto-vegetarian diet. We do not eat meat, fish or eggs. But all dairy products and honey are fine to consume.

6.5.3 Vedic Etiquette (Shishtachara)

This is the most important section of the chapter on ethics.

One of the direct extensions of Vedic ethics is what is often called the art of Vedic etiquette (*shishtachara*). Vedic etiquette is not merely a custom of good manners in relating to others. Vedic etiquette is as much an integral part of spiritual practice (*sadhana*) as are Yoga, *pranayama*, *dhyana*, or any other element of practice. It is very much a part of spiritual science and of ethical behavior. It is the Dharma of interpersonal respect. If a person is not practicing Vedic etiquette, then they are not practicing Vedic spirituality at all.

Unfortunately, as the Kali Yuga has progressed, people increasingly made the dire mistake of thinking that Sanatana Dharma was some morally relative, self-opinionated free for all. It is not. We need to have a restoration of respect for, and within, this tradition; a respect that was once the norm, but that has now all but receded into a faint memory for too many people. We must now unapologetically re-teach this science of etiquette to others.

As a prime example among many, it is important that when we address a *guru*, we ask a question, and not merely shout a declarative demand at them. It was with such unfailing respect that I always treated my revered *guru*. If there is some aspect of the tradition of Sanatana Dharma that you do not yet fully understand, then inquire in a humble and respectful manner. But never make the mistake of attacking our religion or the representatives of our religion.

"The symptoms of a *sadhu* are that he is tolerant, merciful, friendly and a well wisher to all living entities. He has no enemies, he is peaceful, he abides by the scriptures, and all his characteristics are sublime." (*Srimad Bhagavatam*, 3.25.21)

"He must always follow the good path that was followed by his ancestors. By doing so, he will never suffer." (Manava Dharma Shastra, *4.178)*

"Having worshipped the gods and sages, and having served the food to the guests and servants, the house holder should take food at the end." (*Manava Dharma Shastra*, 3.117)

"Let him never turn away (a stranger) from his house, that is the rule." (*Taittiriya Upanishad*, 3.10.1)

Contemplation: Above everything else, what motivates us to uphold a proper sense of etiquette toward others is having a healthy service attitude. The Dharmi sees himself as the servant of all beings. He is the servant of his fellow devotees, of his elders, of those whose lives are dedicated to spreading Dharma, to the *guru*, and to God. The natural result of such a humble service attitude is the practice of an active and sincere respect toward all who deserve it.

Guidance: We must especially exercise etiquette and respect toward the *guru*, toward fellow devotees, and to respected elders in the Vedic community.

Exercise: Always respectfully place your hands in *namaskara* gesture (palms together in "prayer pose") and say "Namaste" to your fellow devotees when you attend *satsangha*. This has so much more spiritual meaning and significance than just saying 'hi' or 'hello'.

Principles of Vedic Etiquette

The following are only a small number of the many principles of Vedic etiquette that should be observed by sincere followers of Sanatana Dharma.

ॐ When the *guru* enters the room, it is appropriate to immediately stand in respect if you are in a seated position, or to offer your full obeisances to him by placing your head to the ground before him.

ॐ Respected elders in the community, including especially your own parents and grandparents, should be appreciated for their life-experience, the sacrifices that they have made in their lives, and the wisdom that they have accumulated over the decades.

ॐ It is appropriate to remove your shoes when entering someone's home, a Yoga room, a temple, or any other place where a sacred or spiritual event is occurring.

ॐ Guests to your home should be treated extremely well, and with great respect. At the very least, they should be offered a nice place to sit and a cup of water to drink. They should not be attacked verbally or in any other manner.

ॐ Every time you have finished eating, you should then immediately rinse your hands and your lips with clean water.

ॐ When speaking to someone who is not an enemy, make eye contact and display a pleasant countenance.

ॐ Do not write on the pages or page margins of a sacred scripture.

ॐ Do not allow your children to run or to be overly boisterous and loud in a sacred place.

ॐ Never recline or lie down in a temple or while at a *satsangha* gathering. Either sit or stand.

ॐ Never sit on a seat that is elevated higher than the *guru's* seat.

ॐ Do not argue or engage in contentious debates with others.

ॐ Always observe natural hierarchy in all social relations. Show great respect to those who are above you spiritually, socially or in age. Be friendly, accessible and cordial to those who are on your same level. Give guidance, advice, and a good example to those who are below you.

ॐ Always reply courteously in friendly situations with such normative courteous phrases as "thank you", "you're welcome", etc.

Third Wave - Socio-Historical Grounding

In this section of the book *Sanatana Dharma: The Eternal Natural Way*, we conduct comparative analyses of Sanatana Dharma with several other world religions. We also examine some of the historical and present-day challenges that the eternal Vedic tradition has faced, and the solution to those challenges.

Chapter 7 Comparing Religious Traditions

While there is some natural overlap in the philosophical teachings and in
the spiritual practices that are found among all the major world religions,
Sanatana Dharma is very different from any other religion in the world
today. Sanatana Dharma represents the most ancient and intact spiritual
tradition on Earth. It is the very expression of the cosmos itself. That
being the case, it forms the very foundation of religion itself. Because this
is the case, while offering respect and tolerance of all the later religions
that came into being historically, Sanatana Dharma recognizes itself as
occupying the very apex of all spiritual and religious phenomena. In
chapter seven, we explore some of the similarities and differences between Sanatana Dharma and a few of the more prominent world
religions that came after it.

"All those traditions and all those disreputable systems of philosophy
that are not based on the *Veda* produce no positive result after death; for
they are declared to be founded on darkness. All those doctrines differing
from the *Veda* that spring up and soon perish are ineffectual and mis-
leading, because they are of modern date." (*Manava Dharma Shastra*,
12.95)

> Question: Can you list three ways in which Sanatana Dharma is
> very different from every other religion in the world today?

7.1.1 Sanatana Dharma and Buddhism

In understanding the relationship between Sanatana Dharma and Buddhism, it is important to understand that there are actually two forms of
Buddhism that are found historically. There is 1) the Buddhism that con-

sists of the original teachings of the Buddha, and there is 2) the more contemporary Buddhism that represents a gradual falling away from those original teachings.

Gautama Buddha was a royal prince who renounced his kingdom in order to become a Vedic *yogi* and devote himself to the search for Truth. He himself never declared that he was teaching something new, or trying to establish a new religion outside of the Vedic understanding. The Buddha himself was never a Buddhist! Rather, he was situated within a Vedic cultural and spiritual context for the totality of his life. He practiced Sanatana Dharma for all of his life. And he left this world as a follower of Sanatana Dharma.

Buddha's original teachings were non-different from Sanatana Dharma, but with the slight nuances that a) he emphasized the Yoga tradition and downplayed the ritual tradition; b) he taught via a process of negation, in other words, by what Truth is not, more so than what actually Truth is. Otherwise, all the Vedic spiritual teachers of his day completely accepted the Buddha as another teacher within the Vedic tradition.

Buddhism became dogmatized and rigidified as a separate religion by the emperor Ashoka (circa 304-232 BCE). It also became philosophically compromised by Nagarjuna (circa 150-250 AD) with the introduction of the false ideas of 1) no permanent self, 2) no Absolute and 3) Shunyata (Nothingness).

Followers of Sanatana Dharma accept the original and unaltered teachings of the Buddha as non-different from Sanatana Dharma, but reject much of contemporary Buddhism in its now altered form. Sincere followers of the Buddha who wish to fully understand and practice his teachings should explore the Buddha's personal spiritual tradition: Sanatana Dharma. Studying the book *Sanatana Dharma: The Eternal Natural Way* is a good way to begin that process.

"Both formally and now, I have never been a nihilist, never been one who teaches the annihilation of a being. Rather, I have taught only the source of suffering, and its ending." (Gautama Buddha, *Majjhima Nikaya*, 1.140)

> Questions: The essence of the Buddha's teaching is that all beings are experiencing suffering. The goal of life is to cease all suffering by achieving *nirvana* – a Vedic word meaning "enlightenment". If there is no real and permanent self, then who is it who is experiencing suffering? What is the purpose of seeking the enlightenment and liberation of a non-existent being?

> Fact: The beliefs that a) there is permanent self, b) yet there is a self who is suffering and who needs to become enlightened are mutually contradictory. There either is a self who is suffering and needs enlightenment, or there is not.

7.2.1 Jesus: The Dharma Master

Similar to the distinction that we see between original Buddhism versus contemporary Buddhism, we recognize that there have been two very distinct trends within the 2000-year-old Christian tradition. These are:

a) Paleo Christianity
b) Pauline Christianity

Simply put, the first represents the original teachings and practices of the great Dharma teacher Jesus. The latter represents the corruption of those original teachings and practices as expressed in modern mainstream Christianity.

Jesus was not a Christian. He never claimed that he was. The term "Christianity" itself came about long after Jesus was no longer living. Jesus was a Dharma Master. His original teachings were non-different from those of Sanatana Dharma. In order to fully understand and practice the teachings of Jesus in a truly pure and authentic manner, it will be necessary for contemporary followers of Jesus to completely reject all traces of Abrahamism that have corrupted the original teachings of Jesus for the last two millennia.

Such a re-embrace of Jesus' original message entails a thorough rejection of the Old Testament and the god of the Old Testament, as well as the rejection of the fallacies of Paul in the New Testament. It means reintroducing the concepts of reincarnation, vegetarianism, meditation, mysticism and Gnosis (positive spiritual knowledge) that Jesus himself followed and taught. Only upon such an exorcism of the evils of Abrahamism will 'Christians' truly understand the authentic teachings of Christ.

"What you seek after (is) within you." (*The Dialogue of the Savior*)

"Jesus said, "If your leaders say to you, 'Look, the (Father's) kingdom is in the sky,' then the birds of the sky will precede you. If they say to you, 'It is in the sea,' then the fish will precede you. Rather, the (Father's) kingdom is within you and it is outside you. When you know yourselves, then you will be known, and you will understand that you are children of

126

the living Father. But if you do not know yourselves, then you live in poverty, and you are the poverty." (*Gospel of Thomas*, 3)

"Beware that no one lead you astray, saying 'Lo here!' or 'Lo there!' For the Son of Man is within you. Follow after him! Those who seek him will find him." (*The Gospel of Mary*)

"This soul needs to follow another soul in whom the Spirit of life dwells, because she is saved through the Spirit. Then she will never be thrust into flesh again." (*The Secret Book of John*, 14.20)

> Guidance: Pauline Christians claim that it is enough to simply "accept Jesus as your Lord and Savior" in order to attain spiritual emancipation. Yet there is the famous story of the rich man who had complete faith in Jesus. He completely accepted Jesus as his "Lord and Savior". Nonetheless, Jesus rejected this man because he could not follow in the actual footsteps of Jesus. He could not **do** as Jesus was doing. (Matthew, 19.24) Jesus, thus, proves with his own words and actions the mainstream Christians wrong when they say that it is sufficient to simply "accept Jesus as your Lord and Savior". Blind faith alone is not enough. It is easy to worship Jesus, but it is very difficult to actually do as he did – which is what he wants us to do. We must do as Jesus did, follow his path, become like him. We must become *yogis* thoroughly absorbed in God-consciousness. Sanatana Dharma shows us exactly how to do this.

7.3.1 Sanatana Dharma and Islam

Of all the world religions in existence today, Sanatana Dharma and Islam represent polar opposites in every way.[18] Sanatana Dharma represents the essence of Natural Law, and the origin of all natural religions throughout

---

[18] Philosophically, however, Marxism represents the complete opposite of Sanatana Dharma.

history. Sanatana Dharma fosters such values as reason, balance, nobility, inclusiveness, tolerance, and compassion. The religion of Islam, on the other hand, is the epitome of the Abrahamic mindset and praxis. Islam is predicated upon such pathologies as irrationality, alienation, barbarity, exclusiveness, intolerance and violence. Therefore, unlike the two religions discussed above (Buddhism and Paleo-Christianity), Islam is considered to be *adharma*, or the very opposite of Dharma.

"Having a form of a ghost (*bhuta*), the expert illusionist Muhammad (Mahamada) appeared at night in front of King Bhojaraja and said: 'O king, your religion is of course known as the best religion among all. Still I am going to establish a terrible and demoniac religion by the order of my god. The symptoms of my followers will be that they first of all will cut their genitals (circumcision), have no *shikha* (a tuft of hair on the back of the head that many Vedic priests have), but having beard, they shall be wicked, make noise loudly and eat any kind of food. They should eat animals without performing any rituals. This is my opinion. They will perform purificatory act with the *musala* or a pestle as you purify your things with *kusha*. Therefore, they will be known as Musalman, the corrupters of religion. The demonic religion will be thus founded by me.' After having heard all this the king came back to his palace and that ghost (Muhammad) went back to his place." (*Bhavishya Purana*, 3.3.5-27)

Though the following quote is not from the Vedic scriptures, but from the writings of the 11th century Islamic writer Abu Rayhan al-Biruni, it supports from an Islamic perspective the fact that Islam and Sanatana Dharma represent polar opposites in the realm of spirituality.

"They [Dharmis] totally differ from us [Muslims] in religion, as we believe in nothing in which they believe, and vice versa." (al-Biruni, *al-Hind*)

Guidance: The Vedic tradition does not believe in persecuting or harming people simply because they follow a different path from ours. Followers of Sanatana Dharma uphold the principle of non-violence (*ahimsa*) by extending our compassion to all living beings, human and non-human. We understand Nature to be an extension of God's mercy and wisdom. As such, we have the deepest reverence for Nature and Nature's laws. Islam, on the other hand, is a religio-martial force that sees itself as being in a violent war with the entire world.

7.4.1 The Abrahamic World-view Versus the Dharmic World-view

Previous to the period of the last two thousand years, the Dharmic (natural) view of reality was the predominant world-view upon the Earth. Most of the nations of the world attempted to order their governments, cultures and sciences in accordance with Dharma (Natural Law). With the arising of Abraham on the world scene, however, a brand new, anti-natural world-view was unleashed upon the Earth, the primary goal of which was to overturn and replace everything Dharmic with the new ideology of Abrahamism.

Abrahamism has led to the creation of several distinct movements over the course of human history, including Judaism, Pauline Christianity, Islam and Marxism.[19] The greatest geopolitical, philosophical, cultural and spiritual conflicts that have been witnessed for the last 4000 years of human history have been nothing more than the conflict between these two radically distinct and opposing systems of Dharma and Abrahamism.

---

[19] The Baha'i movement and Luciferianism (including all followers of Aleister Crowley) are also denominations of Abrahamism.

"Under no circumstances can the words of persons bewildered by illusion deviate the intelligence of those who are completely surrendered souls." (*Srimad Bhagavatam*, 3.2.10)

"Adam (Arda), Noah (Nogha), and Abraham (Vardht) [are the first three barbarian teachers]; there are also five others whose nature is tamasic (darkness) in the family of demonic snakes: Musa (Musa), Isa (Isha), the White-Clad One (Shvetavastrin), Muhammad (Madhupati), and the Mahdi (Mathant), who will be the eighth – he will belong to the darkness. The seventh will clearly be born in the city of Baghdad in the land of Mecca (Makha), where the demonic incarnation - the mighty, merciless idol of the barbarians - lives in the world." (*Sri Kalachakra Tantra*, 1.5)[20]

> Exercise: In order to live a more Natural Law based lifestyle, slowly and systematically begin removing all Abrahamic influences from your life. Give your children Sanskritic Vedic names, not Biblical or Quranic ones. Avoid eating or using any products ritually offered to Yahweh or Allah (kosher or hallal). Immerse yourself in the Vedic scriptures, in Vedic etiquette and lifestyle, and in Vedic cuisine. In this way, you will be increasingly living in accordance with the Natural Way. The result will be that you will experience a new peace, radiance, health, energy and fulfillment that you only dreamed possible previously.

7.4.2 The Abrahamic World-View

This section reveals several of the shared elements of the three the Abrahamic religions (Judaism, Christianity and Islam). This is only a small list:

1. Acceptance the Old Testament.
2. Biblical anthropomorphic monotheism.
3. Religious exclusivity.
4. Belief that theirs is the only true faith.
5. Violence, terror and aggressive missionary tactics to spread

---

[20] Even though the *Kalachakra Tantra* is officially a Buddhist scripture, it describes in exacting detail the differences between Dharma and Abrahamism.

their religion.

6. Being at a war with the Dharmic world.

7. Prayer rather than meditation.

8. The existence of fallen angels, the devil, demonic spirits, etc.

9. The bodily resurrection, the Final Judgment, the post-natal creation of the soul, the binding effects of sin, etc.

10. One specific day of the week set aside for prayer and rest.

"An illiterate barbarian (*mleccha*) teacher will appear, Mahamada is his name, and he will give religion to his fifth-class companions." (*Bhavishya Purana*, 3.3.3. 5-6)

Guidance: Sanatana Dharma teaches the either opposite or non-existence of most of the above-shared elements of Abrahamism.

The following list is a comparison of some of the elements of Dharma and Abrahamism.

The Dharmic and Abrahamic World-views

DHARMA	ABRAHAMISM
Pro-Nature	Anti-Nature
Tolerant	Intolerant
Integrative	Conflictual
Inclusivistic	Exclusivistic
Not Patriarchal	Patriarchal
Divinity is Masculine/Feminine	Divinity is Exclusively Masculine
Qualitative Values	Quantitative Values
Cyclical	Linear
Panentheistic Monotheism	Anthropomorphic Monotheism
Compassion	Legalism
Mercy	Law
Natural	Artificial
Art	Science
Omnisentiency	Anthropo-sentiency
Ethno-Pluralism	Ethno-Chauvinism
Beauty Revered	Beauty Feared
Women Respected	Women Oppressed
Vegetarian	Carnivorous
Rational	Emotional
Organic	Synthetic
Virtue	Morality
Acknowledgement of Lesser Divinities	Yahweh/Allah Only
Peaceful	Warlike
Non-imperialistic	Imperialistic
Philosophical	Dogmatic
Literate	Non-literate
Pre-denominational	Denominational

"O lotus-eyed Lord, although non-devotees who accept severe austerities and penances to achieve the highest position may think themselves liberated, their intelligence is impure. They fall down from their position of imagined superiority because they have no regard for Your lotus feet." (*Srimad Bhagavatam*, 10.2.32)

> Exercise: Can you think of any other ways in which Sanatana Dharma and Abrahamism differ from each other?

7.5.1 2000 Year Genocide Against Dharma

While the Abrahamic assault against Dharma began with Abraham some 4000 years ago, the genocidal practices of the followers of Abraham were at first limited only to the geographic area of Palestine up until the birth of Pauline Christianity.

With the arising of Pauline Christianity as a political force in Europe, however, the Abrahamic movement now acquired the power of the Roman state apparatus to wage their genocidal war on a global scale. It was beginning in the first 300-400 years after the birth of Christianity that we began to see the conquering of entire nations, and even empires, by the imperialistic forces of Judaism, Pauline Christianity and Islam.

Though it is true that Dharma began its gradual receding of influence starting with the commencement of the Kali Yuga, beginning 3102 BCE, the systematic eradication of entire Dharma civilizations did not begin until approximately 2000 years ago.

"Now the sinful Kali Age is upon them, when Dharma is destroyed, an Age full of evil customs and deceit. Men pursue evil ways. The *Vedas* have lost their power, the *Smritis* are forgotten, and many of the *Puranas*, which contain stories of the past, and show the many ways (which lead to liberation), will, O Lord! be destroyed. Men will become averse from religious rites..." (*Maha-Nirvana Tantra*, 1.37-39)

> Exercise: If you were a follower of one of the Abrahamic religions previous to practicing Sanatana Dharma, it is certain that at some point in history your ancestors were converted to one of these Abrahamic religions either by force or pressure. What was your ancestors' religion before being converted to an Abrahamic religion? Research your family's history and the original religion of your ancestor's people to discover the answer to this question. For example, if you are of Irish origin, your ancestors' original religion was probably the Druid religion of the ancient Celtic people. During your next *puja* or meditation, honor those pre-Abrahamic ancestors of yours and tell them that you have now re-embraced the Natural Way. Tell them that you have now spiritually come home to them.

7.5.2 Twelve-Hundred Years of Battering

Sanatana Dharma in its purely Vedic form finally began coming under direct assault on the sub-continent of South Asia[21] around the 9th century. This was a war against Dharma that lasted for 1200 years, and that has taken the lives of at least 100 million South Asian Dharmis. That war against Dharma continued into the 21st century under the auspices of the atheist Congress Party regime in India. 2014 has marked the end of such persecution of Vedic civilization in India with the election, for the first time since Indian independence, of a pro-Sanatana Dharma Prime Minister and Parliament.

---

[21] South Asia includes: India, Pakistan, Afghanistan, Nepal, Bhutan, Bangladesh, Sri Lanka, and usually Tibet.

"But the land that lies between those two mountains (Himavat and Vindhya), which extends as far as the eastern and the western oceans, the wise call Aryavarta (the nation of the Noble Ones)." (*Manava Dharma Shastra*, 2.22)

> Questions: Have you ever been discriminated against due to your adherence to Dharma? Do you know others who have been similarly persecuted?

Chapter 8: Sanatana Dharma Today

Chapter eight examines the current state of Sanatana Dharma globally

(but with a special emphasis on America), and the factors that are leading

to a coming historic period that I have termed Dharmodaya, or Dharma

Ascending.

"The Chakravartin (universal Dharma leader) shall come out at the end of the age, from the city the gods fashioned on Mount Kailasha. He shall smite the anti-Dharmic barbarians in battle with his own four-division army, on the entire surface of the earth." (*Sri Kalachakra Tantra*, 1.161)

> Question: What signs have you seen in society that point to a revival of Vedic and Dharmic spirituality?

8.1.1 The Current Global Crisis

The world of the early 21st century has become a place of many crises,

including economic, political, cultural and civility crises. These crises,

though affecting people on a material level, find their ultimately source in

the fact that our secular, materialist era has abandoned all semblance of real spiritual life. Society has lost all sense of meaning and higher purpose. The Sanatana Dharma movement holds the greatest promise as the force that will bring about a global spiritual restoration.

"Sukadeva Gosvami said: Then, O King, Dharma, truthfulness, cleanliness, tolerance, mercy, duration of life, physical strength and memory will all diminish day by day because of the powerful influence of the Age of Kali." (*Srimad Bhagavatam*, 12.2.2)

"A person's spiritual position will be ascertained merely according to external symbols, and on that same basis people will change from one spiritual order to the next. A person's propriety will be seriously questioned if he does not earn a good living. And one who is very clever at juggling words will be considered a learned scholar." (*Srimad Bhagavatam*, 12.2.5)

Question: What are some of the other negative symptoms of the Kali Yuga that you have yourself witnessed?

8.1.2 Dharma and Spiritual Empowerment

So many leaders of our society seem powerless to bring about the changes necessary to make our world sane and functional again. This is because such leaders are lacking in the positive spiritual empowerment necessary to create real and lasting change in society. It is in cultivating a strong spiritual practice in our lives, and drawing ourselves closer to God as our Source, that we will find the empowerment necessary to help ourselves, and to transform our world for the better. It is through Dharma that we will recover our inner strength, courage, nobility and self-discipline.

"With the sword of Knowledge, armed with Yoga, slay the doubt in the heart born out of ignorance. Stand and fight." (*Bhagavad Gita*, 4.42)

<u>Questions</u>: From where do you derive your empowerment?
What great leaders have served as inspirations to you?

8.1.3 Dharma Ascending

It is Dharma that forms the basis of all meaningful civilization. Having gone through the period of darkness that we have all experienced in recent centuries, we will now experience the restoration of Dharma again. This is known as Dharmodaya, the age of Dharma Ascending.

"Therefore, get up! Prepare to fight and earn glory! Conquer our enemies and take delight in a flourishing Dharma Imperium. The enemies of Dharma are already vanquished by My arrangement. You, O Arjuna, can be but an instrument in the fight." (*Bhagavad Gita*, 11.33)

<u>Question</u>: In what areas of society have you seen positive indications that an increasing number of people are becoming empowered to practice and teach Dharmic ways?

8.2.1 Sanatana Dharma's Contributions to the New Age Movement

The American New Age movement has grown in recent decades to alter the entire spiritual landscape both in America and globally. Most of the foundational practices of the New Age movement have been directly borrowed (many would say stolen!) from the much more ancient Vedic tradition, but without much of the credit given to the Vedic tradition. Whether we are speaking of Yoga, meditation, *chakras*, *kundalini*, reincarnation and *karma*, natural medicine, Ayurveda, *mantras*, *mandalas*, etc., these are not "New Age" ideas and practices at all. These practices were not born in the 1960s, and have nothing to do with Hippie or alternative American culture. They are all completely Vedic in origin.

In addition to the New Age movement pirating all of these elements directly from Sanatana Dharma, and without giving any credit to the original spiritual culture from which it was taken, many of these sacred elements have been altered and misused for commercial reasons. It is for this reason that followers of Sanatana Dharma need to begin speaking out boldly in educating the public to the fact that they need to begin to explore the Vedic tradition if they wish to understand all of these spiritual arts and technologies in their true, authentic and most effective form. It is time for New Age people to abandon the imitation, and explore the original.

"People who are erroneous and bewildered by the illusory energy will give up the original Dharma and its principles and guidance. Abandoning character, cleanliness and neglecting the Supreme Lord, they will accept nonsensical teachings. Following concocted spiritual paths, accepting pseudo spiritual vows in accordance with their own desires, they will abound. During this Age of Kali, people are more inclined to anti-Dharmic (*adharma-bahulena*) systems. Consequently these people, whose pure consciousness is destroyed, will naturally deride the Vedic tradition, the followers of Vedic authority, Vedic ritual, the *brahmanas*, the Supreme Godhead and the devotees." (*Srimad Bhagavatam*, 5.6.10)

> Discussion: Why are the following New Age statements not taken seriously either by followers of Sanatana Dharma or by thoughtful followers of any other legitimate spiritual tradition?
>
> "We are all one."
> "Follow your own truth."
> "I am my own *guru*."
> "Everything is God."
> "Nature is God."
> "You are God/I am God."

"All paths are one."
"Love of yourself is the greatest love of all."
"We're all special."
"I am spiritual, not religious."
"We're all the same."
"It doesn't matter what you believe or do."
"We all have our own truth."

Please analyze and critique these New Age statements in light of the teachings of the Vedic scriptures and the Acharyas.

8.3.1 Bridging the Gap: Indian Hindus and Western Dharmis

There are two distinct Sanatana Dharma communities in America and Europe. These are 1) Indian Hindus, and 2) Western practitioners of Yoga and Vedic spirituality. Indian Hindus tend to consciously identify with Sanatana Dharma, and take part in the rich temple and ritual culture of Vedic spirituality. They rarely, however, actually practice Yoga, meditation or in-depth study of Vedic philosophy.

Western Yogis and Dharmis, on the other hand, tend to practice Yoga and meditation, and to study Vedic philosophy, but they rarely publically identify Sanatana Dharma as their spiritual tradition, or take part temple and ritual culture. Each group must learn what it is lacking from the other in order for both communities to become fully practicing and self-identified members of the Sanatana Dharma family.

Questions:

For Western Yogis: Have you ever visited a Hindu/Vedic temple; performed a *puja*; or hosted a home *satsangha*? What is your religion? How do you identify yourself religiously?

For Indian Hindus: Do you meditate daily? How often do you practice Yoga? Have you studied the *Bhagavad Gita*, the major *Upanishads*, and the *Brahma Sutras*?

8.4.1 Does Sanatana Dharma Have a Future in America?

From sections 8.4.1 to 8.4.8 of the book *Sanatana Dharma: The Eternal Natural Way*, we explore the history of Sanatana Dharma in America, as well as some of the challenges that Sanatana Dharma faces. We also discuss the increasing popularity of everything yogic and Vedic in the West, and what the future holds for our tradition.

Dharmo rakshati rakshitaha

"Those who defend Dharma are likewise protected by Dharma." (*Mahabharata*, 3.312.128)

Discussion: Is being in America a hindrance or a help in practicing Sanatana Dharma?

8.5.1 The Sun of Dharma Arises in the West

In our current age, the Sun of Dharma has been setting in Asia, only to beginning arising with ever-increasing brilliance in the Western world. The practice of Yoga, meditation, natural healing, and other aspects of Dharma are being increasingly embraced by many people in the West. This will lead to the eventual creation of a beautiful Dharma civilization in the West.

140

Yato dharmah tato jayah

"With Dharma there is victory!" (*Mahabharata*, 6.65.18)

Question: What can I do to help ensure the continued growth of Dharma in the world?

Fourth Wave - Grounding in Practice

The fourth and final wave of the *Nectarean Ocean of the Eternal Natural Way*[22] brings the philosophy of Sanatana Dharma to life in the form of personal practice. In this last section, we look at many of the forms of meditation, Yoga, and other *sadhanas* that are foundational for the serious practitioner.

---

[22] Which is the alternative name of the book *Sanatana Dharma: The Eternal Natural Way*.

142

Chapter 9: Taking Refuge in Dharma

Chapter nine focuses on how a person enters the Sanatana Dharma tradition, and commences the path of spiritual practice under the guidance of a qualified *guru*.

9.1.1 Why Should I Be a Dharmi?

The beginning of Vedic spiritual life begins with consciously identifying oneself as a Dharmi. If a person is not even comfortable with making the statement that "My religion is Sanatana Dharma", then how much true commitment can a person put into the actual practice of this path? It is only possible to fully identify with this tradition if one understands the many reasons why it makes sense to follow Sanatana Dharma.

The Vedic path is a holistic and comprehensive lifestyle that benefits us in many ways, including spiritually, in our personal health and wellbeing, and in helping to transform the world around us into a much better place. The many benefits of practicing Sanatana Dharma are seen when one begins to follow the Dharma lifestyle.

Beginning a Dharma lifestyle includes the following:

1. Becoming vegetarian.

2. Starting to read the Bhagavad Gita and other Vedic texts under the guidance of someone who fully understands the teachings of the scriptures.

3. Reading the books "*Sanatana Dharma: The Eternal Natural Way*" and "*Living Dharma*".

4. Practicing authentic meditation techniques, especially medita

tion upon the *mantra* **Aum Namo Narayanaya**.

5. Understanding the basic philosophy of Dharma and accepting the principles of *karma*/reincarnation.

6. Becoming a member of the International Sanatana Dharma Society, the premier organization teaching Vedic spirituality in the world today.

As one progresses along the Dharmic path, and is eventually ready to become a more serious spiritual practitioner, the following additional elements can be added to one's Dharma lifestyle.

1. Seeking initiation from a qualified *guru* (spiritual teacher). Please get a copy of the book *Taking Refuge in Dharma* for more information on precisely how to go about the process of taking initiation from a qualified *guru*.

2. Strictly observing the ethical principles of Dharma.

3. Practicing spiritual meditation, *puja* and other *sadhanas* on a daily basis under the expert guidance of a qualified *guru*.

4. Becoming an active volunteer for the International Sanatana Dharma Society.

9.2.1 Choosing Sanatana Dharma as One's Spiritual Path

A very frequent question that people will often ask is, how does a person formally accept Sanatana Dharma as their chosen religious tradition? Interestingly, unlike many other religions, there is no formal conversion process for entry into Sanatana Dharma. Dharma is the Natural Way. That being the case, how does a person "convert" to the way of nature? This was a question that the *rishis* never had to even think about because at the time when they were operating in our world, there was no other religion in existence other than the Eternal Natural Way! There was really nothing to convert to or from. Rather than speaking in terms of conversion, it is understood that a person is either living in accordance with nature, or they are not. They are either Dharmic or adharmic (anti-Dharmic).

Thus, a person is considered a formal follower of Sanatana Dharma as soon as he accepts Sanatana Dharma within his heart as his chosen path. In this way, a person's acceptance of Sanatana Dharma as their path is a very personal experience that happens in different ways, and at different life-stages, for different people. The only welcoming ritual that may be interpreted as a possible official welcoming ceremony is the formal initiation process that a serious practitioner undergoes upon the acceptance of a *guru*, or spiritual teacher. Otherwise, all good and sincere people are welcome to formally adopt the tradition of Sanatana Dharma as their chosen spiritual path.

> Questions: When did you begin to feel that Sanatana Dharma was your own personal spiritual home? What occurred at the time to help you make the decision to adopt Sanatana Dharma as your own spiritual tradition?

> Fact: Some of the most important figures in recent history were either followers of, or greatly inspired by, Vedic spirituality. These include: Arthur Schopenhauer, Ralph Waldo Emerson, Henry David Thoreau, Nikola Tesla, Romain Rolland, Nicholas Roerich, Chistopher Isherwood, Erwin Schrödinger, JD Salinger, George Harrison, Julia Roberts, Russell Brand, and Congresswoman Tulasi Gabbard, among many hundreds of other well-known figures.

9.3.1 The Importance of the Guru in Sanatana Dharma

It is no exaggeration to say that the most important process in the practice of serious Vedic spirituality (as opposed to a more "New Age" or faddish approach to Vedic spirituality) is the acceptance of a personal *guru* as one's trusted spiritual guide and mentor. The *guru* must be a presently living person who has attained full self-realization and God-consciousness, and who has been empowered by his own *guru* to teach others.

To find a true and authentic *guru* today is an extreme challenge. At least 95% of people today who portray themselves as either *gurus* or enlightened spiritual teachers are actually not.[23] Thus, finding a truly liberated being to serve as one's *guru* is the most precious of honors, and is a rare privilege that should be fully appreciated.

> *tad viddhi pranipatena pariprashnena sevaya*
> *upadekshyanti te jnanam jnaninas tattva-darshinah*

"Just try to learn the Truth by approaching a spiritual master. Inquire from him submissively and render service unto him. The self-realized soul can impart knowledge unto you because he has seen the Truth." (*Bhagavad Gita*, 4:34)

> *janana-maranadi-samsaranala-santapto dipta-shira jala-rasim iva*
> *upahara-panam sotriyam brahma-nishtham gurum upasrtya tam anusarati*

"Just as a person whose head is on fire runs to water, one who burns from the flames of birth, death, old age, and disease in the holocaust of

---

[23] Many of these unethical people, who pose themselves as *gurus* before they are ready to do so, suffer from what I have termed Premature Guru Syndrome.

material existence must run to a genuine *guru* for relief. Such a *guru* must be fixed in the Absolute Truth and well versed in the scriptures. One should approach him with all that is needed for sacrifice and submit to him as a disciple, ready to carry out his every instruction." (*Vedanta-Sara*, 11)

> *tasmad gurum prapadyeta jijnasum shreyam uttamam*
> *shabde pare cha nishnatam brahmany upasamasrayam*

"One who is searching for the Ultimate Truth must surrender unto a spiritual master, a *guru*. A *guru* knows the inner meaning of the *Vedas*, is fixed in the Absolute Truth and is expert in the *shastra*, the revealed scriptures." (*Bhagavata Purana*, 11.3.21)

> *achinoti yam shastrartham achare sthapayaty api*
> *svayam acharate yasma acharyas tena kirtitam*

"An Acharya is one who fully understands the conclusions of the revealed scriptures. His own behavior reflects his deep realization, and thus he is a living example of divine precept. He is therefore known as an Acharya, or one who teaches the meaning of the scriptures both by word and deed." (*Vayu Purana*)

> *acharyam mam vijaniyam navamanyeta karhicit*
> *na martya buddhyasuyeta sarva-deva mayo gurum*

[Krishna told Uddhava] "Know the Acharya as My very Self. I am the Acharya. Never envy the Acharya; never blaspheme him or consider him to be an ordinary man. Because the Acharya channels the infinite, He is greater than the sum total of all the finite. Thus, he is more important than all the gods." (*Srimad Bhagavatam*, 11.17.27)

> *yasya sakshad bhagavati jnana-dipa prade gurau*
> *martyashad-dhim shrutam tasya sarvam ku-jara-shaucavat*

"The *guru* must be considered to be like the Supreme Lord Himself, because he bestows the light of transcendental knowledge upon his disciples. Consequently, for one who maintains the material conception that the *guru* is an ordinary human being, everything is frustrated. His attempts to make progress in spiritual life - his Vedic studies and scriptural knowledge, his penances and austerities, and his worship of the deideity - are all as useless as the bathing of an elephant who rolls in the mud after his bath." (*Srimad Bhagavatam*, 11.20.17)

naivopayanty apachitim kavayas tavesha
brahmayusapi krtam rddha mudam smaruntam
yo'ntar bahis tanu-bhrtam asubham vidhunvann
acharya-chaittya vapusa sva-gatim vyanakti

[Uddhava said to Sri Krishna] "O my Lord! Transcendental poets and experts in spiritual science could not fully express their indebtedness to You, even if they were endowed with the lifetime of Brahma, for You appear in two features - externally as the Acharya and internally as the Paramatman, the Supreme Self - to deliver the embodied living beings by revealing to them your devotional service and teaching them how to approach you on the path of divine love." (*Srimad Bhagavatam*, 11.29.6)

shravanayapi bahubhir yo na labhyam
shrnvanto 'pi bahavo na vidyum
acharyo 'sya vakta kushalo 'sya labhda
acharyo jnata kushala nushishtam

"Many cannot even hear about the soul, and even after hearing about the soul, many cannot understand it; this is because it is hard to find an Acharya who is a genuine seer of the truth. Such a qualified Acharya is a great soul and is very rare. At the same time, realization of the truth can be had only by those disciples who carefully follow the qualified Acharya's teachings and become expert in the science of God. Such disciples are also very rare. Thus it is that only a few ever come to know the soul in truth." (*Katha Upanisad*, 1.2.7.)

"Persons who are strongly entrapped by the consciousness of enjoying material life, and who have therefore accepted as their leader or guru a similar blind man attached to external sense objects, cannot understand that the goal of life is to engage in the service of Lord Vishnu. As blind men guided by another blind man miss the right path and fall into a ditch, materially attached men led by another materially attached man are bound by the ropes of fruitive labor, which are made of very strong

148

cords, and they continue again and again in materialistic life, suffering the threefold miseries." (*Srimad Bhagavatam*, 7.5.31)

Characteristics of the True Guru:

What constitutes a true *guru* is not a mystery in any way. The Vedic scriptures are filled with detailed descriptions of what a person's behavior must be like if they claim to be a *guru*. Below is just a small sample of some of the characteristics of a true *guru*.

*sri-bhagavan uvacha
prakasham cha pravrttim cha moham eva cha pandava
na dveshti sampravrttani na nivrttani kankshati*

*udasina-vad asino gunair yo na vichalyate
guna vartanta ity evam yo 'vatishthati nengate*

*sama-duhkha-sukhah sva-sthah sama-lostasma-kanchanah
tulya-priyapriyo dhiras tulya-nindatma-samstutih*

*manapamanayos tulyas tulyo mitrari-pakshayoh
sarvarambha-parityagi gunatitah sa uchyate*

"The Blessed Lord said: He who does not hate illumination, attachment and delusion when they are present, nor longs for them when they disappear; who is seated like one unconcerned, being situated beyond these material reactions of the modes of nature, who remains firm, knowing that the modes alone are active; who regards alike pleasure and pain, and looks on a clod, a stone and a piece of gold with an equal eye; who is wise and holds praise and blame to be the same; who is unchanged in honor and dishonor, who treats friend and foe alike, who has abandoned all fruitive undertakings--such a man is said to have transcended the modes of nature." (*Bhagavad Gita*, 14.22-25)

"The Blessed Lord said: Fearlessness, purification of one's existence, cultivation of spiritual knowledge, charity, self-control, performance of sacrifice, study of the Vedas, austerity and simplicity; nonviolence, truthfulness, freedom from anger; renunciation, tranquility, aversion to fault-finding, compassion and freedom from covetousness; gentleness, modesty and steady determination; vigor, forgiveness, fortitude, cleanliness, freedom from envy and the passion for honor--these transcendental qualities, O son of Bharata, belong to godly men endowed with divine nature." (*Bhagavad Gita*, 16:1-3)

Guidance:

A true *guru*: a) is a fully liberated being; b) has extensive knowledge of the Vedic scriptures; c) has incomparable knowledge of both Vedic spirituality and philosophy, and of the ideological systems that oppose Vedic philosophy (the *purva-pakshas*); d) has the ability to teach; e) is a moral and ethical person in all of his or her thoughts, words and conduct; f) personifies the teachings of Dharma in his or her behavior; g) is initiated in a recognized and authentic Vedic lineage (*sampradaya*); h) has the ability to spiritually empower his or her disciples.

A fraudulent *guru*: a) suffers from Premature Guru Syndrome, that is, they begin to act in the role of a spiritual teacher before they have even allowed themselves to progress past the neophyte stage as a practitioner; b) is not a fully liberated being; c) engages in sexually predatory behavior, often under the excuse of practicing "Tantra"; d) claims to be "beyond good and evil" before they have even approached what it means to be good, and as a justification to commit evil; e) propitiates and celebrates dark and evil entities; f) craves power, both material and "spiritual"; g) supports the fallacy of Radical Universalism (stating that "all religions are the same"); h) allows his disciples to worship him as an *avatara*, or an incarnation of God; i) cannot demonstrate any connection to a legitimate Vedic lineage (*sampradaya*); j) is motivated by wealth, greed, anger and lust.

Fact: A true *guru* can be either a man or a woman. Gender is not a bar to a person performing the duties of a *guru*.

150

9.4.1 The Art of Questioning

Sanatana Dharma is a tradition in which we are encouraged to ask perti-
nent philosophical questions. There is, however, a fine art and etiquette
to questioning that must be understood and applied if you are to derive
the maximal benefit from the *guru's* presence. It is when we ask our questions with openness, humility, patience, and sincerity that we are then
able to receive valuable answers from the *guru* that we are then empowered to incorporate into our lives.

When, on the other hand, we ask in a mood of arrogance, showmanship,
unconstructive skepticism, or with the idea that we are either equal to, or
in competition with, the *guru*, then we have constructed a perceptual wall
around our intellects through which the light of Truth will not penetrate.
In approaching a *guru*, it is important to choose our words and our mood
wisely. Otherwise, rather than having opened ourselves to making spiritual progress, we have only committed an offence toward the very
person who is in a position to help us make progress.

"To that pupil who has duly approached him, whose mind is completely
serene, and whose senses are controlled, the wise teacher should indeed
rightly impart the knowledge of Brahman, through which one knows the
immutable and the true God." (*Mundaka Upanishad*, 1.2.13)

Manushyam sahasreshu kashchid yatati siddhaye
Yatatam api siddhanam kashchin mam vetti tattvatah

"Of many thousands of men, one will attempt to reach perfection; and of
the few who reach this goal, only a rare soul will perhaps know Me as I
am." (*Bhagavad Gita*, 7:3)

"Those words which do not describe the glories of the Lord, who alone
can sanctify the atmosphere of the whole universe, are considered by

saintly persons to be like unto a place of pilgrimage for crows. Since the all-perfect persons are inhabitants of the transcendental abode, they do not derive any pleasure there." (*Srimad Bhagavatam*, 1.5.10)

> Guidance: The proper way to ask a *guru* a question includes the following steps. When in a large group setting, begin by politely addressing the *guru* with a formal title, "Guru Maharaja", "Acharyaji", "Gurudeva", etc. Address your inquiry in the form of a question, not just a comment or propositional statement. Listen with great attention and awareness to the answer to your question. Reflect upon the answer, allowing not only the words of the *guru* to enter your ears, but allowing the Truth that the *guru* is conveying to enter your heart. If there is time for follow-up questions, then repeat the above process in asking more questions.

9.5.1 The Process of Diksha

When a person is ready to commence formal study and practice under the guidance of a qualified *guru*, that person then undergoes the process of *diksha*, or initiation by the *guru*. The process of *diksha* is one of the most important milestones in the life of a serious Dharmi, and is not to be taken lightly. The entire process must be approached with the full respect and thoughtful dignity that the procedure deserves. The rest of chapter nine explains the process of initiation in detail.

9.5.2 Requirements for Initiation

We know that the *guru* must meet certain criteria in order to be recognized as an authentic *guru*. In addition to the *guru* meeting the understood requirements to be eligible to bestow initiation, however, the student also needs to fulfill certain requirements in order to be truly ready for this sacred event. These requirements on the part of the student include:

A) Full acceptance of the philosophy of Sanatana Dharma.

B) A full willingness to publicly identify oneself as a Dharmi.

C) Strict vegetarianism (this means no meat, fish or eggs).

D) Following the Yamas and Niyama (the Ten Principles), and all other ethical principles of Sanatana Dharma.

E) Acceptance of the Vedic scriptures as one's ultimate spiritual guide in written form.

F) Acceptance of the principle of *karma* and reincarnation.

G) Sincere and humble acceptance of the *guru* as one's living spiritual guide with faith and devotion.

"The Earth is the place where the Supreme Lord is worshiped, spiritual initiation (*diksha*) is the means of purification for the spirit soul, and rendering devotional service to the Supreme Godhead is the process for eradicating all one's karmic reactions." (*Srimad Bhagavatam*, 12.11.17)

Questions: Can I approach the process of *diksha* with full sincerity, knowledge and commitment? Do I have a healthy trust and faith in the ability of my *guru* to guide me upon the spiritual path? Am I willing to follow the path of Sanatana Dharma exclusively, no longer identifying myself with any other path that I practiced previous to initiation?

9.5.3 Dakshina

An important symbolic aspect of the initiation ritual is giving a gift to the *guru* in thanks for bestowing the initiation. The gift is given as a part of the initiation ritual, and can be anything from a meaningful object, flowers, incense, or a monetary donation.

"O King, those best of persons, Krishna and Balarama, being Themselves the original promulgators of all varieties of knowledge, could immediately assimilate each and every subject after hearing it explained just once. Thus with fixed concentration They learned the sixty-four arts and skills in as many days and nights. Thereafter, O King, They satisfied Their spiritual master by offering him *guru-dakshina*" (*Srimad Bhagavatam*, 10.45.35-36)

> Contemplation: It is in spiritually giving of ourselves with devotion to the higher cause of Dharma that we exercise the opposite attitude of egotism (*ahamkara*).

> Fact: The *guru* does not have an ordinary job or income, as do most people. His entire life is devoted only to serving God, and to teaching others about God. As a full-time spiritual teacher, he is humbly dependent upon the gifts, charity and donations of his students and supporters for his livelihood and to sustain his teaching mission.

9.5.4 The Process of Initiation

When the initiation process takes place at a Sanatana Dharma temple, there is a short fire ceremony that is meant to attract the blessings of the

154

gods and goddesses.[24] After this, the *guru* will bestow upon the student a set of meditation beads (*japa mala*), a set of *tulasi* beads to be worn around the neck, and a spiritual name in Sanskrit, which the new initiate will always be referred by in spiritual circles.[25] The full process is outlined in detail in *Santana Dharma: The Eternal Natural Way*.

> Exercise: Even though *japa mala* beads are traditionally not given to a student for meditation previous to initiation, that does not mean that you should not be meditating daily upon the *mantra* **Aum Namo Narayanaya** previous to receiving your beads. There is always benefit to reciting the sacred names of God, either with or without beads. Try to meditate by reciting the *mantra* **Aum Namo Narayanaya** 108 times each day even if you are not initiated yet.

9.5.5 Guru Pranama Mantra

This is the primary *mantra* used to offer respects to the present Acharya of the International Sanatana Dharma Society.

> *Nama aum vishnu padaya*
> *Krishna preshthaya bhutale*
> *Srimate dharma pravartaka*
> *Acharya iti namine*

---

[24] Under certain circumstances, the fire ceremony can be skipped. The most important element of the initiation ceremony is the taking of vows before the *guru*, and the empowerment that the *guru* gives to the disciple via the *mantra* that is imparted, the *japa-mala* (meditation beads), the *kunti-mala* (neck beads), and the new Sanskrit name given to the new disciple.
[25] Another stipulation is that if the prospective initiate lives in a region or nation that is very far, and cannot travel to the *guru's* location to receive initiation in person, then the *guru* can impart initiation through the mail or even through Skype.

"I offer my respectful obeisances unto he who has taken shelter at the feet of Sri Vishnu, Sri Dharma Pravartaka Acharya, who is very dear to Lord Krishna."

This *mantra* should be recited when offering obeisances to the *guru*, or when making ritual offerings to the *guru* during *puja* and other Vedic ceremonies.

"While engaged in serving the Acharya one should remain as a humble servant, and thus when the *guru* is walking the servant should humbly walk behind. When the *guru* lies down to sleep, the servant should also lie down nearby, and when the *guru* has awakened, the servant should sit near him rendering service to him. When the *guru* is sitting down on his seat, the servant should stand nearby with folded hands, awaiting the *guru's* order. In this way one should always worship the spiritual master." (*Srimad Bhagavatam*, 11.17.29)

> Exercise: Practice reciting the *guru pranama mantra* each day as a daily part of your *sadhana* (spiritual practice) until you feel comfortable in your pronunciation.

9.5.6 Vows Undertaken by the Shishya

During the *diksha* ceremony, the student makes the following vows, which must be thereafter observed strictly and without fail:

- To serve Dharma, God, and Guru with all of your thoughts, words, and deeds.
- To have complete faith and loyalty to the *guru* and the *guru's* mission.
- To meditate on the **Aum Namo Narayanaya** *mantra*, as instructed by the *guru*, each day.
- To be a strict vegetarian.
- To live a Dharma lifestyle to the maximum of your ability.

- To offer compassion to all sentient beings by sharing Dharma with them and helping the *guru* with his mission to teach Dharma to all people to the maximum of your abilities.
- To follow the Yamas and Niyamas, and all the ethical codes of Dharma.

"The mind is like an impetuous horse that even persons who have regulated their senses and breath cannot control. Those in this world who try to tame the uncontrolled mind, but who abandon the feet of their spiritual master (*gurosh-charanam*), encounter hundreds of obstacles in their cultivation of various distressful practices. O unborn Lord, they are like merchants on a boat in the ocean who have failed to employ a helmsman." (*Srimad Bhagavatam*, 10.87.33)

> Guidance: Upon receiving initiation from the *guru*, the disciple now formally enters into a very special relationship with both the *guru*, as well as the fellow disciples of the *guru*. The relationship is that of a spiritual family, or *guru-parivara*. While never replacing the actual biological family, the spiritual family has tremendous significance for the serious practitioner. The *guru* is viewed as the father or mother of the spiritual family, and the fellow initiates are God-brothers and God-sisters.

Chapter 10 Dharma in Practice

Chapter ten reveals several of the deeper and more important spiritual practices that serious followers of the Vedic path should try to observe in their daily lives.

10.1.1 The Inner Dimensions of Sadhana Practice

In addition to the outer form in which we conduct *sadhana* practice, there is an inner element that forms the very heart of spiritual practice. This inner element consists of the four qualities of: sincerity, humility, openness, and yearning for God. It is in cultivating these four qualities that we will know continued success on the spiritual path.

"That which in the beginning may seem just like poison but at the end is just like nectar and which awakens one to self-realization is said to be happiness in the mode of goodness (*sattva-guna*)." (*Bhagavad Gita*, 18.37)

"By one's engaging in the processes of demigod worship, austerities, breath control, compassion, bathing in holy places, strict vows, charity, and chanting of various *mantras*, one's mind cannot attain the same absolute purification as that achieved when the unlimited Godhead appears within one's heart." (*Srimad Bhagavatam*, 12.3.48)

> Questions: How are earnestness and the desire to live a sattvic (good and pure) life reflective of our sincerity? How is humility radically different from humiliation? Does openness mean that we relinquish the ability to use discernment and reason in spiritual pursuit, or does it mean that we open our hearts to Truth? Is it a material desire to yearn for the spiritual?

10.1.2 General Principles of Daily Sadhana

According to the great *rishi* (seer-sage) Patanjali, there are two keys that are essential for success on the spiritual path. These are: *abhyasa* (practice) and *vairagya* (non-attachment).

"Practice (*abhyasa*) is the effort to secure steadiness. This practice becomes well grounded when continued with reverent devotion and without interruption over a long period of time. Desirelessness (*vairagya*) towards the seen and the unseen gives the consciousness of mastery." (*Yoga Sutras*, 1.13-15)

158

In addition, *sadhana* must be practiced in a) thought, b) words and c) action. In this section of the book *Sanatana Dharma: The Eternal Natural Way*, I offer a variety of guidelines in which we can deepen our *sadhana* in thought, words and action. Of these many guidelines, the following are the most important.

Ya vai sadhana-sampattih purushartha-chatushtaye
Taya vina tad apnoti naro narayanashrayah

"Whatever among the four goals of human life[26] can be achieved by various spiritual practices is automatically achieved without such endeavors by the person who has taken shelter of Lord Narayana, the refuge of all persons." (*Mahabharata, Shanti Parva [Mokshadharma Parva], Narayaniya*)

1. Each day, we should meditate upon the names of Śriman Narayana for a minimum of one round on a *japa mala* (meditation beads) made of *tulasi* wood.

2. Each day we must strive to increasingly deepen our understanding of our *gurudeva's* teachings, to assist his teaching mission with enthusiasm, and to offer our devoted respects to him.

3. Observe a proper spiritual diet by eating vegetarian and sattvic foods.

4. Study the sacred Vedic literatures very systematically and reverently.

5. Have an altar in your home where you keep a sacred image (*murti*) of Lord Krishna, or other forms of the Lord.

6. Every day offer compassion to others by helping them spiritually.

---

[26] The four goals of life (known as the *purusha-arthas* in Sanskrit) are: 1) *dharma*, 2) *artha* (material prosperity), 3) *kama* (material pleasure), and 4) *moksha* (liberation).

7. Associate with like minded devotees and develop their godly qualities. This is good association (*satsangha*).

8. Give up unhealthy habits such as smoking, drinking and taking drugs, and instead replace them with the spiritually beneficial habits of service (*seva*).

9. As followers of Dharma, we are called upon to strive toward ethical excellence.

10. Always try to offer practical service (*seva*) to God in accordance with your capacity, means, skills, and understanding.

11. Learn to spiritualize your speech by speaking truth at all times.

12. Always think of Lord Krishna, as awareness of God is the essence of all scriptural injunctions.

"Studying the *Vedas* and acquisition of knowledge, practicing austerities (*tapas*), not engaging in violence against others, serving the *guru*, and establishing effective control over the senses are acts which secure the highest good to a person." (*Manava Dharma Shastra*, 12.83)

> *yoga-sthah kuru karmani sangam tyaktva dhananjaya*
> *siddhy-asiddhyoh samo bhutva samatvam yoga ucyate*

"Be steadfast in yoga, O Arjuna. Perform your duty and abandon all attachment to success or failure. Such evenness of mind is called Yoga." (*Bhagavad Gita*, 2.48)

> *jatasya hi dhruvo mrtyur dhruvam janma mrtasya ca*
> *tasmad apariharye 'rthe na tvam socitum arhasi*

"For one who has taken his birth, death is certain; and for one who is dead, birth is certain. Therefore, in the unavoidable discharge of your duty, you should not lament." (*Bhagavad Gita*, 2.27)

"Devotional consciousness alone is the most precious possession of a person who is truthful in his thoughts, words, and actions." (*Narada Bhakti Sutras*, 81)

Questions: What can I do to inspire myself to practice my *sadhana* every day? How can being too attached to the outcome of even spiritual practice end up holding us back?

Guidance: Use your thoughts in *sadhana* by always thinking about the divine lotus feet of Bhagavan Sri Krishna. Use your words by always teaching others about Dharma. Employ your power of action always in the transcendental service of God and Guru.

10.2.1 Yoga: The Heart of Sanatana Dharma

Tens of millions of Americans and Europeans are now practicing Yoga. For most of these practitioners, however, Yoga is not much more than an exotic series of physical exercises. A large minority of these Western *yogis*, though, does understand that Yoga is primarily a spiritual path. The path of Yoga is nothing less than Sanatana Dharma in practical application. When you are practicing Yoga for spiritual purposes, you are practicing Sanatana Dharma. The goal of Yoga is twofold: 1) self-realization (*atma-jnana*) and 2) God-consciousness (*brahma-vidya*).

The authentic Yoga system is found primarily within the pages of the *Upanishads* and the *Bhagavad Gita*. This original Yoga system is the eight-limbed (*ashtanga*) Yoga system (later written about by the famous sage Patanjali in his *Yoga Sutras*), infused throughout with *bhakti* (devotional consciousness). The eight limbs of the authentic Yoga system are:

Yama: Five positive ethical guidelines.

Niyama: Five positive behaviors.

Asana: Physical exercises designed to give our bodies strength, flexibility and energy in order to engage in longer periods of meditation.

Pranayama: Breathing exercises that produce vitality, overall health, inner calm, and greater integration between the physical and subtle bodies.

Pratyahara: Detachment from the ever-present fluctuations of life, leading to an increasing interiorization. *Pratyahara* is a bridge between the physical and the mental aspects of the human person.

Dharana: The practice of powerful and focused concentration.

Dhyana: Devotional meditation on God.

Samadhi: This is blissful absorption of one's individual consciousness in the essence of God.

We are meant to practice all eight limbs of Yoga simultaneously, and in a state of pure devotion.

"By steady knowledge a sage should clearly ascertain the nature of the soul's bondage and liberation. Bondage occurs when the senses are deviated to sense gratification, and complete control of the senses constitutes liberation." (*Uddhava Gita*, 13:22)

"The wise person [the *yogi*] should hold his body steady, with the three [upper] parts erect, turn his senses, with the help of the mind, toward the heart, and by means of the raft of Brahman cross the fearful torrents of the world." (*Shvetashvatara Upanishad*, 2.8)

Exercise: The next time that you practice *asanas* (physical Yoga poses), either at a Yoga class or at home, coordinate the flow from *asana* to *asana* with a full awareness of your breath. Begin your *asana* practice by first performing *mantra* meditation, and end with a deep *shavasana* session. As you are in the midst of the *asanas*, cultivate an attitude of devotional surrender to God with each pose.

10.3.1 Meditation – The Heart of Yoga

In the modern world, when we hear the term "Yoga", we tend to think almost immediately of only the system of physical exercises associated with the practice. The *asanas*, however, do not constitute the essential practice of Yoga. Rather, meditation is the heart of Yoga. Yoga exists for the stilling of the mind, which is only achievable through the process of meditation. From sections 10.3.1 to 10.3.4, we explore the exact process of meditation as practiced in the authentic Yoga system of the Vedic scriptures.

yogash chitta vritti nirodhah

"Yoga is the stilling of the modifications of the mind." (*Yoga Sutras*, 1.2)

"One-pointedness is steadfastness of the mind. Unbroken continuation of that mental ability is meditation." (*Yoga Sutras*, 3.1-2)

"Brahman is not grasped by the eye, nor by speech, nor by the other senses, nor by penance or good works. A man becomes pure through serenity of intellect; thereupon, in meditation, he beholds Him who is without parts." (*Mundaka Upanishad*, 3.1.8)

> Guidance: Meditation is the conscious awareness of an object using one-pointed focus and concentration. Meditation is only truly meditation if we are willingly meditating with a purpose.

This is why daydreaming or "zoning out" are not meditation. Meditation produces sharp awareness, not unwilling drowsiness.

10.3.2 Beginning Meditation with Breath Concentration

Focusing your attention upon your breath is a wonderful way to relax, to rid yourself of tension and anxiety, and to allow the mind to become still. By focusing all of our awareness on breath, we are harmonizing breath, body and mind in a natural and peaceful way. There are also more advanced breathing techniques, known as *pranayama*, that can help even more in achieving complete control of your mind.

Breath concentration alone is not the most powerful or spiritual form of meditation, however, because it only affects us on the physical and mental level. It only produces physical and mental relaxation – but not spiritual realization. It is specifically with the introduction of God's name (*harinama*) into our meditation session that the transcendental, and thus spiritual, element is now being practiced in meditation.

tasmin sati shvasa prashvsayoh gati vichchedah pranayama

"After perfection of posture is achieved, the movements of inhalation and exhalation should be controlled. This is *pranayama*." (*Yoga Sutras*, 2.49)

"The *yogi* of well regulated endeavors should control the *pranas*; when they are quieted he should breathe out through the nostrils. Then let him undistractedly restrain his mind, as a charioteer restrains his vicious horses." (*Shvetashvatara Upanishad*, 2.9)

164

Exercise: A simple form of breath concentration consists of sitting in lotus position (half-lotus position, *ardhapadma asana*, is just
as good) in a quiet place with your eyes closed, and beginning to
bring your full awareness only to the reality of your own breathing. Breathing in a normal and rhythmic way, filling your belly
with breath, begin to feel and hear the sound of your own
breath. Allow yourself to sink deeper and deeper in relaxation as
you focus your mind on nothing but breath.

10.3.3 Mantra – Meditation Upon God's Name

There are several different forms of meditation that have been used by

successful *yogis* for thousands of years. Of all these different meditation

practices, however, the most effective and spiritual form of meditation is

mantra meditation – meditating directly upon the divine names of God.

This form of meditation is the most effective because God's name is

non-different from God (which is not the case with our names). God and

God's names are both eternal and absolute. Therefore, when God's name

is present upon our lips, He is Himself present before us. Through *mantra*

meditation, we can have the most intimate and vivid experience of God's

presence within us.

"One who desires to be free from all miseries must hear about,
glorify, and also remember the supreme lord, who is supersoul, the
controller and the savior from all miseries." (*Srimad Bhagavatam*, 2.1.5)

Guidance: The only true and effective *mantras* are those *mantras*
that are directly revealed in the Vedic scriptures. A person cannot just make up a *mantra*, or use a mundane word to meditate
upon and simply call it a *mantra*. A *mantra* has to have been an
eternal sound vibration that was revealed by a *rishi* (seer-sage)
and recorded in a Vedic scripture. More, not even all *mantras* that
are revealed in the Vedic scriptures necessarily have spiritual liberation as their goal. There are different specific *mantras* for

different specific purposes. Those *mantras* that contain the names of God within them are especially meant for spiritual liberation.

10.3.4 How to Meditate

There are several recommendations for creating the right environment for a positive meditation experience. These include having a clean, un-cluttered space where you meditate regularly; sitting with your back in a straight, yet comfortable, position; sitting either on the floor or on a meditation cushion; and patiently working on focus, concentration and awareness. Breath concentration helps with the last part.

"Select a clean spot, neither too high nor too low, and seat yourself firm-ly on a cloth, a deerskin, and *kusha* grass. Then, once seated, strive to still your thoughts. Make your mind one-pointed in meditation, and your heart will be purified. Hold your body, head, and neck firmly in a straight line and keep your eyes from wandering. With all fears dissolved in the peace of the Self and all desires dedicated to Brahman, controlling the mind and fixing it on Me, sit in meditation with Me as your only goal." (*Bhagavad Gita*, 6:11-14)

> *duhkheshv anudvigna-manah sukheshu vigata-sprhah*
> *vita-raga-bhaya-krodhah sthita-dhir munir uchyate*

"One who is not disturbed in spite of the threefold miseries, who is not elated when experiencing pleasantness, and who is free from attachment, fear and anger, is called a sage of steady mind." (*Bhagavad Gita*, 2:56)

> *tad-buddhayas tad-atmanas tan-nishthas tat-parayanah*
> *gacchanty apunar-avrttim jnana-nirdhuta-kalmasah*

"When one's intelligence, mind, faith and refuge are all fixed in the Su-preme, then one becomes fully cleansed of misgivings through complete knowledge and thus proceeds straight on the path of liberation." (*Bhaga-*

166

vad Gita, 5.17)

man-mana bhava mad-bhakto mad-yaji mam namaskuru
mam evaishyasi satyam te pratijane priyo 'si me

"Always think of Me and become My devotee. Worship Me and offer your homage unto Me. Thus you will come to Me without fail. I promise you this because you are My very dear friend." (*Bhagavad Gita*, 18.65)

Questions: What is your personal meditation area like? Is it a sacred space where you feel that you can get away from the many distractions of daily life?

10.3.5 Mantra Meditation

The most effective way to practice meditation is to have a full and consistent *mantra* meditation session each day. A full *mantra* meditation session consists of three parts:

A) 2-5 minutes silent breath concentration.

B) 10-15 minutes of out loud chanting of *Aum Namo Narayanaya*.

C) 2-5 minutes of silent breath concentration again.

The actual timing of each part can be either increased or decreased.[27] But the important thing is to follow this three-fold sequence:

Breath Mantra Breath

---

[27] While the quality of one's meditation experience is of foremost importance, the quantity is of importance as well. So the longer one can meditate for, the better.

The Mantra

The most powerful and effective of *mantras* that we can use in our meditation is revealed in the Vedic scriptures as the *mantra*:

ॐ नमो नारायणाय

Aum Namo Narayanaya

The literal translation of this effective and empowering *mantra* is *"I offer my obeisances to that Absolute who is the Sustainer of All Beings."*

"That yogi who meditates on 'Aum Namo Narayanaya' attains Vaikuntha, the anxiety-free abode of Lord Vishnu." (*Narayana Upanishad*, verse 4)

"Oh mortal beings, you have submerged yourselves fully in the ocean of material existence, which is filled with the waves of misfortune. Please hear as I briefly tell you how to attain your supreme benefit. Just put aside your various attempts at gaining knowledge and instead begin constantly chanting the *mantra* 'Aum Namo Narayanaya' and bowing down to the Lord." (*Mukunda Mala Stotra*, 16)

Guidance: If you are just beginning your meditation practice, slowly increase the amount of time that you meditate each day. If it is difficult for you to meditate for 20-30 minutes right away, then start with ten minutes each day, and slowly increase the duration. It is better to meditate for ten minutes every single day than to meditate for half an hour every other day. The key to success in meditation is consistency. Make sure that your meditation practice is a daily practice.

Additional Mantras

In addition to the Narayana *mantra* mentioned above, there are several other Vedic *mantras* that can also lead one to God-consciousness. These are only a few of them. We have provided a beautifully produced CD containing many of these *mantras* so you can practice perfecting your pronunciation at home. The CD is available at Dharmacentral.com

    1) Aum Namo Bhagavate Vasudevaya

    2) Aum Ventateshaya Namaha

    3) Aum Vishnave Namaha

    4) Aum Sri Krishnaya Namaha

    5) Aum Namo Bhagavate Narasimhaya

    6) Aum Sri Maha-Lakshmyai Namaha

    7) krishnaya vasudevaya
      devaki-nandanaya cha
      nanda-gopa-kumaraya
      govindaya namo namah[28]

    8) Hare Rama Hare Rama / Rama Rama Hare Hare
      Hare Krishna Hare Krishna / Krishna Krishna Hare Hare[29]

---

[28] Translation: "Let me therefore offer my respectful obeisances unto the Lord, who has become the son of Vasudeva, the pleasure of Devaki, the boy of Nanda and the other cowherd men of Vrndavana, and the enlivener of the cows and the senses." (*Srimad Bhagavatam*, 1.8.21)

[29] This is actually the correct way to recite this Vedic *mantra*. The Hare Rama section comes first, followed by the Hare Krishna section. Saying the Hare Krishna portion first, then followed by the Hare Rama portion, was an alteration that occurred in the early 18th Century. There is spiritual benefit, however, whichever way one says the *mantra* because it is composed of three names of God.

The three primary ways in which *mantra* meditation can be performed is either a) to say the *mantra* outloud so that others can clearly hear it, b) to whisper the *mantra* so that only you can hear it as the reciter, or c) to repeat the *mantra* in your mind. Each proceeding way of reciting the *mantra* is more effective than the last, but is also more difficult for the meditator.

"Devotional consciousness (*bhakti*), beginning with meditating upon the holy name of the Lord, is the ultimate Dharma for the living being in human society." (*Srimad Bhagavatam*, 6.3.22)

> *harer nama harer nama harer namaiva kevalam*
> *kalau nasty eva nasty eva nasty eva gatir anyatha*

"In this Kali Yuga (Age of Conflict) the only means of achieving liberation is meditating upon the holy name of Lord Hari, the holy name of Lord Hari, the holy name of Lord Hari. There is no other way. There is no other way. There is no other way." (*Brhad Naradiya Purana*, 38.126)

"Yama said: The goal which all the *Vedas* declare, which all austerities aim at, and which men desire when they lead the life of continence, I will tell you briefly: it is Aum. This syllable Aum is indeed Brahman. This syllable is the Highest. Whosoever knows this syllable obtains all that he desires." (*Katha Upanishad*, 1.2.15-16)

> *sa hovaca hiranyagarbah*
> *hare rama hare rama, rama rama hare hare*
> *hare krishna hare krishna, krishna krishna hare hare*
>
> *iti shodashakam namnam, kali-kalmasha-nashanam*
> *natah parataropayah, sarva-vedeshu drishyate*

"Lord Brahma replied, 'The sixteen words - **Hare Rama, Hare Rama, Rama Rama, Hare Hare Hare Krishna, Hare Krishna, Krishna Krishna, Hare Hare** - are especially meant for completely destroying all the contamination of the Kali Yuga. This is the only destroyer of contamination in Kali-yuga. No other remedy can be found in all of the Vedic literature.'" (*Kali-Santarana Upanishad*, 5-6)

"The *japa yajna*, or the sacrifice of chanting on beads, is basically of three kinds. The differences in these three kinds of *japa* can be elucidated as follows. The first kind of *mantra japa* is known as *vachika* (loud) *japa*, the second is called as *upanshu* (whispering) *japa* and the third is known as *manasa* (mental) *japa*." (*Nrisimha Purana*, 155)

> Question: You have a name that was most likely given to you by your parents. That name, however, is relative. It was given to you at a certain point in time, and it could have easily been a different name that was given to you. At what point in time, however, was God given His name?

> Guidance: Since God is eternal and absolute, God's name is co-eternal and co-absolute with God. There was never a time in which we could say that God was "given His name". For this reason, God's name is not relative like your name, or the name of any material object. This is why, when we meditate upon the names of God, God is Himself present. Unlike any other name in existence, God's name has the ability to heal us, and to lead us to spiritual enlightenment.

10.4.1 Bhakti: The Heart of Meditation

There are two forms of meditation:

> A) Mental Meditation, in which we are using meditation to achieve calm and stillness of our body and mind.

> B) Spiritual Meditation, in which we are discovering our true self, and experiencing the presence of the Divine.

It is the latter form of meditation that is the entire purpose of the Yoga system. Only spiritual meditation fulfills the ultimate goal of meditation. The goal of all authentic spiritual pursuit is to achieve a state of devotional consciousness (*bhakti*) in meditative absorption upon the Divine.

In devotional consciousness (*bhakti*), the liberated *yogi* eternally enjoys the state of loving reciprocal union with God. This is perfect *samadhi* (*asamprajnata samadhi*).

> *yoginam api sarvesham mad-gatenantar-atmana*
> *shraddhavan bhajate yo mam sa me yuktatamo matah*

"Of all *yogis*, he who always abides in Me with great faith, worshiping Me in transcendental devotional consciousness, is most intimately united with Me in Yoga and is the highest of all." (*Bhagavad Gita*, 6:47)

> *purushah sa parah partha bhaktya labhyas tv ananyaya*
> *yasyantahsthani bhutani yena sarvam idam tatam*

"The Supreme, who is greater than all, is attainable by devotional consciousness. Although He is present in His abode, He is all-pervading, and everything is situated within Him." (*Bhagavad Gita*, 8:22)

> *mat-karma-krn mat-paramo mad-bhaktah sanga-varjitah*
> *nirvairah sarva-bhuteshu yah sa mam eti pandava*

"One who is engaged in devotion to Me, free from the contaminations of previous activities, who is friendly to every living entity, certainly comes to Me, O son of Pandu." (*Bhagavad Gita*, 11:55)

"The supreme Dharma for all humanity is that by which men can attain to devotional consciousness unto the transcendent Lord. Such devotional service must be unmotivated and uninterrupted to completely satisfy the self." (*Srimad Bhagavatam*, 1.2.6)

"Let me offer my respectful obeisances unto the all-auspicious Lord Sri Krishna again and again because the great learned sages, the great performers of charity, the great workers of distinction, the great philosophers and mystics, the great chanters of the Vedic hymns and the great followers of Vedic principles cannot achieve any fruitful result without dedication of such great qualities to the service of the Lord." (*Srimad Bhagavatam*, 2.4.17)

172

<u>Questions</u>: What are some of the many reasons that a person will begin a meditation practice? Can all the positive results of mental meditation also be achieved by performing spiritual meditation? Do we also achieve calm, elimination of stress, inner peace, a sharper mind, better concentration, and a rich inner life when we meditate directly upon the Supreme Absolute?

10.4.2 Bhakti Yoga

Bhakti Yoga is considered to be the supreme form of Yoga by all the Vedic scriptures. *Bhakti* (devotional consciousness) is both a process of Yoga, as well as the very goal of all Yoga. This makes the path of *bhakti* radically different from all other forms of Yoga, all of which are processes only. Bhakti Yoga consists of the practice of the entire *ashtanga* (eight limb) system of Yoga, permeated throughout with an ever-increasing degree of devotional consciousness toward God. The perfection of Yoga is to be found in practicing the *ashtanga* system while simultaneously cultivating a constant consciousness of devotion during one's practice.

> *tesham satata-yuktanam bhajatam priti-purvakam*
> *dadami buddhi-yogam tam yena mam upayanti te*

"To those who are constantly devoted and worship Me with love, I give the intelligence by which they come to Me." (*Bhagavad Gita*, 10:10)

> *mam cha yo 'vyabhicharena bhakti-yogena sevate*
> *sa gunan samatityaitan brahma-bhuyaya kalpate*

"One who serves Me in the Yoga of devotional consciousness, unfailing in all circumstances, at once transcends the modes of material nature and thus comes to the level of Brahman." (*Bhagavad Gita*, 14.26)

<u>Exercise</u>: Observe the Yamas and Niyamas out of devotion to the Supreme Godhead. As you perform your *asanas*, peacefully recite the Aum Namo Narayanaya *mantra* within your mind as you gently flow from pose to pose. When you are doing *pranayama*, visualize that you are filling your lungs with God's grace as you inhale, and ridding yourself of lust, anger and greed with each exhalation. As you practice withdrawing the senses from the external world (*pratyahara*) and entering the inner domain of your heart, know that you encountering the very seat of God within. Use an image of God (Narayana or Krishna) as your focal point of concentration (*dharana*). Meditate upon the sacred names of God as you practice *dhyana*. Experience small glimpses of your intimate union (*samadhi*) of love with God throughout the day.

10.4.3 The Descent of the Infinite

All the scriptures of Sanatana Dharma are in agreement with the fact that the Supreme Being is known as Sriman Narayana (sometimes also as Vishnu, which is another name of Sriman Narayana). Though God is completely transcendent in relation to materiality and the material world, He can and does periodically descend into the material realm of His own free will at times when Dharma is so acutely under assault that nothing less than God's direct intervention can restore Natural Order to the cosmos. Such descents of the Divine are known as the manifestation of an *avatara*. The two primary forms of such *avataras* are:

1) *Purna-avatara*, or a full incarnation of God Himself.

2) *Avesha-avatara*, or an instance in which a human being is fully empowered directly by God to restore Dharma in this world.

174

An *avesha-avatara* is so infused with God's grace that it is considered that God is fully present within, and acting through, such a person.

Sri bhagavan uvacha
bahuni me vyatitani janmani tava charjuna
tany aham veda sarvani na tvam vettha parantapa

"Many, many births both you and I have passed. I can remember all of them, but you cannot..." (*Bhagavad Gita*, 4:5).

yada yada hi dharmasya glanir bhavati bharata
abhyutthanam adharmasya tadatmanam shrjamyaham
paritranaya sadhunam vinashaya cha dushkrtam
dharma-samsthapanarthaya sambhavami yuge yuge

"Whenever and wherever there is a decline in Dharma, O descendent of Bharata, and a predominant rise of the opposite of Dharma (*adharma*) - at that time I descend Myself. In order to deliver the pious and to annihilate the evil, as well as to reestablish the principles of Dharma, I advent Myself millennium after millennium." (*Bhagavad Gita*, 4:7-8)

Krishnas tu bhagavan svayam

"Krishna [Narayana] is God Himself" (*Srimad Bhagavatam*, 1.3.28)

"Anyone, even a person in an impure state, who absorbs his mind in Lord Krishna for just a moment at the time of death burns up all traces of karmic reactions and immediately attains the supreme transcendental destination in a pure, spiritual form as effulgent as the sun." (*Srimad Bhagavatam*, 10.46.33)

"The Lord appeared in His original form, with ornaments and weapons in His hands. Although this ever-existing form is not visible in the material world, He nonetheless appeared in this form. Then, in the presence of His father and mother, He assumed the form of Vamana, a *brahmana*-dwarf, a *brahmachari* (celibate student), just like a theatrical actor." (*Srimad*

Bhagavatam, 8.18.12)

A Partial List of Avesha Avataras

> Narada Muni
> Rishabha Maharaja
> Badarayana Vyasa
> Nammalvar
> Gautama Buddha
> Jesus Christ
> Ramanuja Acharya
> Chaitanya Mahaprabhu
> Sahajananda Swami (Swaminarayana)
> Bhaktivedanta Swami Prabhupada

> Guidance: According to the Vedic scriptures, the next full (*purna*) *avatara* of God is Kalki. He will be appearing upon our planet more than 425,000 years from now. There will be no other full *avataras* within the Kali Yuga between now and when Kalki arrives. Any *guru* who claims to be an *avatara* is making a fraudulent claim and is to be rejected as a liar.

10.4.4 The Difference Between Devotion and Emotion

Periodically, less knowledgeable authors will falsely state that Bhakti Yoga is "the Yoga of emotions". Nothing could be further from the truth. Devotional consciousness, or *bhakti*, has absolutely nothing to do with material emotions or emotionality. Emotions are materially derived expressions that may be either good or bad, but which are materially originated nonetheless.

While the *yogi* does not believe in artificially repressing emotions, still mundane emotions arising from illusion are to be transcended through the process of *nishkama*, or a healthy sense of detachment from material worries. Emotion is self-indulgence. Devotion is self-surrender. *Bhakti* is descriptive of a systematic philosophy and means of achieving God-consciousness, as well as a liberated mode of consciousness. Bhakti Yoga is not "the Yoga of emotions".

sa tv asmin parama-prema-rupa

"Devotional consciousness manifests as the most elevated, pure love for God." (*Narada Bhakti Sutra*, 2)

ye tu sarvani karmani mayi sannyasya mat-parah
ananyenaiva yogena mam dhyayanta upasate

tesham aham samuddharta mrtyu-samsara-sagarat
bhavami na chirat partha mayy aveshita-chetasam

"For one who worships Me, giving up all his activities unto Me and being devoted to Me without deviation, engaged in devotional consciousness and always meditating upon Me, who has fixed his mind upon Me, O son of Prtha, for him I am the swift deliverer from the ocean of birth and death." (*Bhagavad Gita*, 12.6-7)

"Let me offer my repeated obeisances unto the all-auspicious Absolute, about whom glorification, remembrances, audience, prayers, hearing and worship can at once cleanse the effects of all negative reactions of the performer." (*Srimad Bhagavatam*, 2.4.15)

"Devotional consciousness is the process of worshiping the Supreme Lord. It consists of fixing one's mind upon Him by becoming disinterested in all material designations, both in this life and the next. This indeed is true renunciation." (*Gopala Tapani Upanishad*, *Purva* 15)

Exercise: The next time that you are afflicted by such negative emotions as anger, envy, worry, depression, lust or fear, try the following practice. If you are in a situation in which you can safely do this, close your eyes and focus all of your awareness on your breathing for at least sixty seconds (even five minutes if you have the time). During this time, do not focus on the source of the negative emotion that you want to overcome. Try to only focus upon your own breath.

If the emotions are still there, observe them as phenomena that are existing outside of yourself. They are like images on a screen in front of you. The images on the screen are not you.

You will witness the negative emotion beginning to fade away. This is because the emotion itself was only an illusion. Once you have witnessed the emotion itself fade away entirely, say the *mantra* Aum Namo Narayanaya three times slowly and outloud (in your mind if you are in public).

In this calm state that you are now experiencing, use your own faculty of wisdom to address the actual problem that caused the debilitating emotion from arising to begin with.

10.4.4 Papatti: The Path of Self Surrender

The most practical expression of *bhakti*, or devotional consciousness, is the process of *prapatti*, complete self-surrender of one's entire being at the feet of God in humility and devotion. Self-surrender to God is the most radical and effective of spiritual paths, since it represents the exact opposite mind-set and activity of *ahamkara*, false ego. With false ego, we are under the illusion that we are the center of all reality. Thus, we act selfishly and self-destructively. With *prapatti*, on the other hand, we acknowledge that God is at the center of all reality. We then act through love toward all beings, and in a way that is spiritually healthy for ourselves. It is in surrendering our self to God that we know and find our true self. It is for this reason that the path of *prapatti* is the highest teaching of the *Bhagavad Gita* (18.66) and of the entire Yoga system.

Prapatti is not merely a one-time act, or some dramatic declaration. Rather, self-surrender is a state of devotional awareness and service toward God that the *yogi* is meant to increasingly cultivate within himself on a daily basis. We continually practice the further deepening of our surrender to God all throughout our life.

> *ye tu sarvani karmani mayi sannyasya mat-parah*
> *ananyenaiva yogena mam dhyayanta upasate*
>
> *tesham aham samuddharta mrtyu-samsara-sagarat*
> *bhavami na chirat partha mayy aveshita-chetasam*

"For one who worships Me, giving up all his activities unto Me and being devoted to Me without deviation, engaged in devotional consciousness and always meditating upon Me, who has fixed his mind upon Me, O son of Prtha, for him I am the swift deliverer from the ocean of birth and death." (*Bhagavad Gita*, 12.6-7)

> *sarva-dharman parityajya mam ekam sharanam vraja*
> *aham tvam sarva-papebhyo mokshayishyami ma shucah*

"Abandon all lesser varieties of religiosity and simply surrender unto Me. I shall deliver you from all negative reactions. Do not fear." (*Bhagavad Gita*, 18:66)

> Meditation: The following prayer from the *Srimad Bhagavatam* perfectly demonstrates the devotional attitude of *prapatti* that the meditator is meant to cultivate within his heart during all spiritual practice. Recite this prayer in both Sanskrit and English before doing your daily meditation upon the *mantra* **Aum Namo Narayanaya** in order to set the proper mood of surrender as you then meditate.

kayena vacha manasendriyair va
buddhyatmana va prakrite-svabhavat
karomi yad yat sakalam parasmai
narayanayeti samarpayami

"Oh Sriman Narayana, I offer to You whatever I do according to my nature, using my body, words, mind, senses, intelligence and purified consciousness. I give all this to You - knowing that it is for Your pleasure." (*Srimad Bhagavatam*, 11.2.36)

10.5.1 The Science of Prayer and Meditation

Praying is a universal practice that we find among all human beings, regardless of their particular religion, and often regardless of whether they even call themselves atheists. Every human being has found himself at some point in his life trying to communicate with a higher power for one reason or another.

"The devotee should offer homage to the Lord with all kinds of hymns and prayers, both from the *Puranas* and from other ancient scriptures, and also from ordinary traditions. Praying, 'O Lord, please be merciful to me!' he should fall down flat like a rod to offer his obeisances." (*Srimad Bhagavatam*, 11.27.45)

Questions: What kind of prayers have you found yourself making at times of trouble? Have you ever prayed to God, not really to ask for anything, but simply to offer Him pure praise?

10.5.2 Prayer in the Sanatana Dharma Tradition

The Vedic literature is richly filled with thousands of beautifully written prayers. The *Rig Veda*, for example, is mostly comprised of prayers. Many of these Vedic prayers can be adopted by us and used in our regular prayer sessions.

> Exercise: Incorporate the following Vedic prayers into your prayer life to better communicate with God in a yogic way.

> *Asato Maa Sad Gamaya*
> *Tamaso Maa Jyotir Gamaya*
> *Mrityor Maa Amritam Gamaya*
> *Aum Shanti Shanti Shantih*

May God lead us from the unreal and to the Real.
May God lead us from darkness to Light.
May God lead us from death to immortality.
Unto all, may peace prevail. (*Brhadaranyaka Upanishad*, 1:3:28)

> *param brahma param dhama pavitram paramam bhavan*
> *purusham shashvatam divyam adi-devam ajam vibhum*
> *ahus tvam rishayah sarve devarshir naradas tatha*
> *asito devalo vyasah svayam chaiva bravishi me*

"You are the Supreme Brahman, the ultimate, the supreme abode and purifier, the Absolute Truth and the eternal divine person. You are the primal God, transcendental and original, and You are the unborn and all-pervading beauty. All the great sages such as Narada, Asita, Devala, and Vyasa proclaim this of You, and now You Yourself are declaring it to me." (*Bhagavad Gita*, 10.12-13)

10.5.3 Diverse Objects of Prayer

Sanatana Dharma is not a polytheistic religion. We do not believe that the Absolute consists of a plurality or a trinity of beings. Even though there are many lesser gods and goddesses in the Vedic pantheon, it is recognized in all the Vedic scriptures that there is ultimately one Supreme

Being who is the source of everything, including all the lesser gods and goddesses (known as *devas* and *devis*, respectively). The *devas* and *devis* are all servants of the Supreme Godhead, and hold a similar position as angels do in modern Western religions.

Sanatana Dharma is a panentheistic religion.[30] We understand that there is ultimately one Absolute who is both thoroughly transcendent, yet simultaneously intimately present in all things. The Supreme Godhead of the Vedic religion is Sriman Narayana. Thus, Sriman Narayana should be the ultimate aim of devotional prayer. The highest prayers are always offered directly to God, Sriman Narayana. It is, however, perfectly acceptable to also offer prayers and supplications to the *devas* and *devis* in order to seek their help in specific ways. The *devas* and *devis* are powerful beings who serve the Supreme Being, and who are there to help us in our spiritual and material advancement. To give an approximate example, God is like the Prime Minister of a nation. The lesser gods and goddesses are like the Ministers of State who serve the Prime Minister.

"Narayana is the totality of the Adityas, Rudras, Maruts, Vasus, Asvins, Rik, Yajus, Sama, Mantras, Agni, and oblation, so also mothers, fathers, etc." (*Subala Upanishad*, 3:4)

"The gods having Vishnu [Narayana] for their chief (who is the perpetual abode of Sri) by the help of (the means prescribed in) the *Vedas* won these worlds for themselves free from the fear of enemies." (*Maha-Narayana Upanishad*, 1:48)

"May the gods who dwell in the highest region of heaven delight me – practicing loving adoration for Vishnu – here on the earth by granting

---

[30] Pane*n*theism is not to be confused with Pantheism. The two words may sound similar, but the philosophical positions they described are irreconcilable.

my wish." (*Maha-Narayana Upanishad*, 2:7)

"All the *devatas* [gods and goddesses] of nature are integral parts of Vishnu." (*Rig Veda*, 1.40.11)

"Like servants, the gods follow Hari [Narayana] who is the Lord of the universe, who leads all thoughts as the foremost leader and who absorbs into Himself the universe at the time of dissolution. May this path to liberation taught in the *Vedas*, having the same form as Brahman, open itself to me. Deprive not me of that. Strive to secure it for me." (*Maha-Narayana Upanishad*, 49:1)

"It was Krishna [Narayana] who in the beginning instructed Brahma (the god of creation) in Vedic knowledge and who disseminated Vedic knowledge in the past." (*Gopala Tapani Upanisad*, 1.24)

"In the beginning of the creation there was only Narayana. There was no Brahma, no Shiva, no water, no fire, no moon, no stars in the sky, no sun." (*Maha Upanishad*, 1)

"Men of small intelligence worship the gods, and their fruits are limited and temporary. Those who worship the gods go to the realm of the gods, but My devotees ultimately reach My supreme abode." (Stated by Sri Krishna - *Bhagavad Gita*, 7:23)

> *yatha-taror-mula-nishechanena*
> *tripyanti tat skanda bhujopashakhah*
> *pranopaharac cha yathendriyanam*
> *tatha cha sarvarhanam achyutejya*

"As the trunk and branches are satisfied by watering the root of the tree and as the life airs are satisfied by offering food to the stomach, all the devatas are worshipped by worship of Achyuta [Narayana]." (*Srimad Bhagavatam*, 4.31.14)

"Lord Krishna is the all-powerful, all-pervading Supreme Godhead, and He is the object of the prayers and worship of the demigods. Intelligent persons worship Him as He resides in his own spiritual abode. They thus attain the eternal transcendental bliss that is not available for others." (*Gopala Tapani Upanishad*, 1.21)

"The dust of Krishna's lotus feet, which is the source of holiness for all places of pilgrimage, is worshiped by all the great demigods." (*Srimad Bhagvatam*, 10.68.37)

"The wise inhabitants of the heavenly regions know that the perfection of the head is to offer obeisances to the Supreme Lord, the perfection of the life-breath is to worship the Lord, the perfection of the mind is to ponder the details of His transcendental qualities, and the perfection of speech is to chant the glories of His qualities". (*Mukunda Mala Stotra*, 46)

> Questions: What is it that you are ultimately seeking spiritually? Are you seeking just any interesting experience that you can then call spiritual? Are you simply seeking power, or the very source of all power? Are you seeking ¼ of the Highest? Or are you truly seeking the very Highest? What you are seeking is what you will find. What you are focusing upon is what you will attain.

10.5.4 The Two Forms of Prayer

Prayer falls under two general categories:

> A) Prayers of appeal, in which we are asking for something material.
>
> B) Prayers of devotional expression, in which the heart is pouring praise upon the Divine in pure love.

While both forms of prayer are positive, prayers of devotion are more important spiritually than any other form of prayer due to the purity of intent. Such prayer is always directed toward God.

The Gayatri *mantra* is a very good example of a prayer directed exclusively toward God.

Gayatri Mantra

Aum bhur bhuvah svah
Tat savitur varenyam
Bhargo devasya dhimahi
Dhiyo yo naha prachodayat aum

> "I invoke the Earth Plane, the Astral Plane, the Plane of Intellect, and the Plane of Absolute Truth. The resplendent effulgence and divine brilliance of God is pure and venerable. We pray and meditate on God to inspire our minds and illuminate our intellect with His divine light."

> Exercise: Recite the Gayatri *mantra* in Sanskrit three times a day: during the morning, at noon, and as the Sun is setting.

"That existence which his teacher, who knows all the *Vedas*, effects for him through the prescribed rites of initiation with the Gayatri is a true existence; that existence is exempt from age and death." (*Vishnu Smriti*, 30.46)

"Fixing the mind on Me, one should worship Me by his various prescribed duties, such as chanting the Gayatri *mantra* at the three junctures of the day. Such performances are enjoined by the *Vedas* and purify the worshiper of reactions to fruitive activities." (*Srimad Bhagavatam*, 11.27.11)

"The Gayatri is everything, whatever here exists. Speech is verily the Gayatri, for speech sings forth (*gaya-ti*) and protects (*traya-te*) everything, whatever here exists. That Gayatri is also the earth; for everything that exists here rests on this earth and does not go beyond." (*Chandogya Upanishad*, 3.12.1-2)

10.5.5 Two-way Communication with God

Prayer and meditation are complimentary practices. Together, they constitute a complete cycle of spiritual practice. Prayer must be coupled with meditation if we are to have a bi-directional communication with God. It is in prayer that we communicate our thoughts, intentions, supplications and praise toward God. Healthy communication, however, is always a two way street. In addition to ourselves speaking to God, we must also be ready to experience God's response. The latter is done through meditation. It is in meditation that we allow the inner whisper of God's loving guidance to speak to us. Thus, a truly rich spiritual life consists of both prayer and meditation.

"If a person hears about, glorifies, meditates upon, worships or simply offers great respect to the Supreme Lord, who is situated within the heart, the Lord will remove from his mind the contamination accumulated during many thousands of lifetimes." (*Srimad Bhagavatam*, 12.3.46)

> Exercise: The next time that you offer prayers to God, follow your prayer with several minutes of silence, in which you open yourself to receiving God's response.

10.6.1 Performing Puja Meditation

One of the most accessible forms of meditation is performing the devotional ritual called *puja*, in which one offers various pure items to an image of God with devotional focus and awareness. The goal of *puja* is not mere ritualism, but the meditative cultivation of self-surrender to

God. In *puja* meditation, we are symbolically offering such items as incense, a flame, water, etc. But with each item that we offer in *puja*, we are meditating upon the fact that we are actually offering ourselves to God. If possible, it is especially recommended that you perform *puja* right before your daily meditation session.

"By worshiping Me through the various methods prescribed in the *Vedas* and *Tantras*, one will gain from Me his desired perfection in both this life and the next." (*Srimad Bhagavatam*, 11.27.49)

"I regard as great even the smallest gift offered by my devotees in pure love, but even great offerings presented by non-devotees do not please Me." (*Srimad Bhagavatam*, 10.81.3)

> Exercise: First perform a brief *puja* at your home altar with devotion. Then, sitting at your altar and smelling the fragrant incense that you just offered to God, perform your daily *mantra* meditation.

10.6.2 Establishing a Home Altar

Whether a family or a single person, every Dharmi household should have an altar in the home where daily *puja*, meditation and *sadhana* take place. Having such an altar in one's home helps to create a spiritual atmosphere, and transforms the home into a temple. May every home be a temple!

"The devotee should more fully establish My Deity by solidly constructing a temple, along with beautiful gardens. These gardens should be set aside to provide flowers for the regular daily worship, special Deity processions and holiday observances." (*Srimad Bhagavatam*, 11.27.50)

Guidance: The altar area should be the heart of every home. It should be in an accessible and central area of the home. Do not be afraid or ashamed to let your guest know that spirituality is central to your life. If you own a house, it is even better if an entire room of the home can be dedicated exclusively to spiritual practice, with the altar placed in that room.

Fact: In the ancient world, it was the norm that every home had an altar in a place of central significance where the entire family and guests could have access to its healing energy. Usually there would be an altar to the primary deity of the home, as well as an altar to the family's ancestors. This was the practice in all of ancient Europe, Asia, the Americas, and Africa.

10.6.3 Conducting Puja

This section provides information on how to perform a simple *puja* ceremony. There are certainly more elaborate *puja* ceremonies that can be performed as well. More elaborate *pujas, yajnas* (fire ceremonies) and other rituals will be published in future books. The most important thing about conducting *puja*, however, is to offer each item on the altar with devotion and love toward the Divine.

"Placing his head at the feet of the Deity, he should then stand with folded hands before the Lord and pray, 'O my Lord, please protect me, who am surrendered unto You. I am most fearful of this ocean of material existence, standing as I am in the mouth of death.'" (*Srimad Bhagavatam*, 11.27.46)

Guidance: It is important to always be aware that *puja* is a meditative exercise, and never just an empty ritual. At every moment that you are performing the *puja*, and with each item that you offer, always keep in the forefront of your mind that you are surrendering yourself to God, and not just the objects that you are offering in ceremony. Always conduct *puja* with great love and devotion toward God.

10.6.4 Puja Mantras

These are some of the *mantras* that should be recited within your mind during *puja*. Recite the following when offering to the *guru*.

> *aum ajnana timirandhasya*
> *jnananjana shalakaya*
> *chakshur unmilitam yena*
> *tasmai sri guruve namaha*

"I offer my respectful obeisances to my spiritual teacher, who has opened my eyes, which were blinded by the darkness of ignorance, with the torchlight of knowledge."

Recite the following in your mind when offering to Krishna/Narayana.

> *he krishna karuna sindho*
> *dina bandho jagat pate*
> *gopesha gopika kanta*
> *radha kanta namo'stu te*

"Oh Krishna, ocean of mercy, You are the friend of the distressed and the source of creation. You are the master of the cowheardmen and the lover of the *gopis*, especially Radha. I offer my respectful obeisances unto You."

Recite the following in your mind as you are offering to Radha/Lakshmi.

tapta kanchana gaurangi
radhe vrindavaneshvari
vrishabhanu sute devi
pranamami hari priye

"I offer my respects to Radha, whose bodily complexion is fair and who is the Queen of Vrindavana. You are the daughter of King Vrishabhanu, and are very dear to Lord Krishna."

Recite this at the end of the puja.

Sriman Narayana Charanau Sharanam Prapadye
Srimate Narayanaya Namah

"I seek refuge at the feet of Sriman Narayana. My salutations to Sriman Narayana."

> Exercise: As you recite these *mantras* in your mind, focus on the subtle mental vibrations produced by each *mantra*. With great devotion, begin to be aware of the vibrations of the *mantras* not only in your mind, but in your heart as well.

10.6.5 Honoring Our Ancestors

All pre-Abrahamic cultures understood the tremendous importance of remaining closely connected to the past if the present was to be invested with any spiritually significant meaning. They also understood that the most personally relevant and accessible portal to the empowering wisdom and goodness of the past was through their own direct ancestors, those who shared their particular bloodline and DNA. It was for this reason that all traditional cultures engaged in what is often called ancestor worship (*pitri-puja*). There is no pre-Abrahamic culture on Earth that did not honor its ancestors in one form or another. This is a very im-

190

portant spiritual practice and tradition that used to be practiced universally by families in the ancient past. The process of ancestor worship now needs to be revived in the modern world if we are to not lose our sacred connection with our own cultural-spiritual heritage. Ancestor worship must become a regular practice again.

"Let there be no neglect of the duties to the Gods and ancestors. Be one to whom mother is God. Be one to whom father is God." (*Taittiriya Upanishad*, 1.11.2)

> Practice: Create another altar, separate from the main altar outlined in the sections above. This can be an altar as simple as a mantle piece, or as elaborate as consisting of a large piece of altar furniture. Once the altar location is decided upon, place photos of your deceased relatives upon this altar – especially photos of relatives and ancestors who you felt close to or inspired by. These must be people who you shared a direct genetic inheritance with (i.e., biological family), and not just anyone. Once a day, make a simple offering of incense to the photos. Then, with your hands in prayer pose, thank them in your mind for their many sacrifices that ensured your family's continuation, for their wisdom and strength, and for their ongoing protection of you and your family. Briefly bow your head toward the ancestors in reverence to end the *pitri puja*.

10.6.6 Where Do I Get Puja Supplies?

The best place to get *puja* supplies, and many other devotional items is www.krishnaculture.com.

10.6.7 The Validity of Murti Meditation

All pre-Abrahamic religions employed the use of sacred imagery as focal points of meditation. Sacred imagery takes many forms, including the use of statuary. Even many Christian denominations use statues and sacred icons as symbols of the Divine, or of various saints and angels. Using sacred imagery is not "idol worship", but a sacred science revealed by God to further our meditative devotion toward Him. This practice is revealed in the Vedic literature as a systematic science in which we employ sacred statues, called *murtis*, as a vehicle through which we can meditate upon, and access, the Divine.

There will always be those who make the claim that "God has no image" or that "God cannot have an image". To say God has no 'x' is to say that God has lack. To say that God cannot have 'x' is, likewise, to say that there are limitations to what God can do. It is to impose a limitation upon God, thus making the Infinite finite. God necessarily has everything, including image. God necessarily can do everything, including making Himself known to us in image form.

Using imagery to worship God is neither primitive, nor putting limitations upon the Divine – being opposed to using imagery is.

"The Deity form of the Lord is said to appear in eight varieties — stone, wood, metal, earth, paint, sand, the mind or jewels." (*Srimad Bhagavatam*, 11.27.12)

"One should worship Me in My Deity forms by offering the most excellent paraphernalia. But a devotee completely freed from material desire may worship Me with whatever he is able to obtain, and may even worship Me within his heart with mental paraphernalia." (*Srimad Bhagavatam*, 11.27.15)

"Whenever one develops faith in Me - in My form as the Deity or in other authentic manifestations - one should worship Me in that form. I certainly exist both within all created beings and also separately in My original form, since I am the Supreme Soul of all." (*Srimad Bhagavatam*, 11.27.48)

> <u>Questions</u>: Even if a person mistakenly believes that God cannot reveal Himself through an image, can God choose to reveal Himself through an image if He so desires? Does God choosing to reveal Himself in a particular image really "limit God"? Does having a photo taken of yourself "limit" who you are as a person and what you can do outside of that photo? Are you more powerful than God?

10.7.1 Eating as Meditation: How to Prepare Prasada

All daily activities can be transcendentalized and used as a meditative tool. This is true even when it comes to the simple act of preparing food and eating. Everyone has to eat. Recognizing this fact, Vedic spirituality even has a way of making eating into a type of meditation!

The word *prasada* means 'mercy'. The practice of manifesting *prasada* is one in which we prepare vegetarian foods in a mood of devotion, eventually offering that food to God upon our home altar or at a temple altar. Once the food is ritually offered in this way, it is now considered to be sanctified and blessed food. It is now called *prasada*, rather than just normal "food". Eating such sanctified food in a mood of meditative devotion is itself a powerful spiritual practice that opens us to the mercy of God.

> *patram pushpam phalam toyam yo me bhaktya prayacchati*
> *tad aham bhakty-upahrtam asnami prayatatmanah*
> *yat karoshi yad asnasi yaj juhoshi dadasi yat*
> *yat tapasyasi kaunteya tat kurushva mad arpanam*

"If one offers Me with love and devotion a leaf, a flower, fruit or water, I will accept it. O son of Kunti, all that you do, all that you eat, all that you offer and give away, as well as all austerities that you may perform, should be done as an offering unto Me." (*Bhagavad Gita*, 9:26-27)

"Even very opulent presentations do not satisfy Me if they are offered by nondevotees. But I am pleased by any insignificant offering made by My loving devotees, and I am certainly most pleased when nice presentations of fragrant oil, incense, flowers and palatable foods are offered with love." (*Srimad Bhagavatam*, 11.27.18)

> <u>Questions</u>: How can you focus your awareness more upon the Divine as you are cooking? Who is responsible for ensuring that the vegetables, fruits, nuts and grains that you eat are filled with life-giving nutritional value and vitality? The farmer grows the food; the grocer sells you the food; you cook the food. But who is ultimately responsible for originating food itself?

10.7.2 Guidelines

There are strict guidelines that must be observed in preparing food to be offered. These guidelines are covered in this section.

"If required, one should endeavor to get sufficient foodstuffs, because it is always necessary and proper to maintain one's health. When the senses, mind and life air are fit, one can contemplate spiritual truth, and by understanding the truth one is liberated." (*Uddhava Gita*, 13:34)

Guidance: When preparing food to offer to God, make sure that every item that you use, as well as your kitchen and you yourself are clean. Do not offer meat, fish, eggs, garlic, onion or mushrooms to God. Do not taste the food until after it is offered.

Contemplation: God is the ultimate source of all food. God is the source of all that is good, healthy, true, and desirable. As we eat and enjoy our food, envision that with every bite and swallow we are filling ourselves with God's radiant, healing love.

10.7.3 How To Offer Food to God

Here we cover the procedure for offering food to God. Please see *Sanatana Dharma: The Eternal Natural Way* for the full process.

"Let him always worship his food, and eat it without contempt. When he sees it, let him rejoice, show a pleased face, and pray that he may always obtain it. Food that is always worshipped gives strength and vigor. But eaten irreverently, it destroys them both." (*Manava Dharma Shastra*, 2.54-55)

Contemplation: Part of what it means to live the lifestyle of a *yogi* is that we approach everything that we do with awareness, being in the moment at all times. This includes maintaining awareness during our daily rituals of eating. Eating can feed both our body and our soul.

10.7.4 Mantras Recited Before Eating

It is a universal practice to offer thanks and acknowledgment before eating our food. Even in the modern Western world, there is at least the notion of saying grace before we eat our food. We should always offer such acknowledgement before starting our meal, whether we are eating alone, and especially when we are eating with others. These are the *mantras* to be said before eating.

Aum bhur bhuvah svah
Tat savitur varenyam
Bhargo devasya dhimahi
Dhiyo yo nah prachodayat aum

Aum Pranaaya Svaaha
Aum Apanaaya Svaaha
Aum Vyanaaya Svaaha
Aum Udanaaya Svaaha
Aum Samanaaya Svaaha[31]

Aum Brahmane Svaaha

Brahmana Atma Amrita Tvaaya.

Amrita api dhaanam asi

("Let this food confer longevity to me.")

Guidance: If we do not have time to say all of these mantras before eating, then we should at the very least say the last one. *Amritaapi dhaanamasi.*

---

[31] These *mantras* are invoking the five *pranas* that operate within our system, giving us vitality and helping us to digest properly, converting food into life-giving energy.

Chapter 11   Living Dharma Today

In this chapter, we discuss the many ways in which a person can help to support Dharma and to share the teachings of Dharma with other people who are in spiritual need. Part of what it means to be a spiritual person is that we have a desire to help others to grow spiritually. To help others spiritually is the most meaningful manifestation of compassion.

11.1.1   Balancing Spiritual and Material Life

Sanatana Dharma is a very practical path in which we are meant to balance our spiritual life with our everyday duties, and not an impractical rejection of the world. The *Bhagavad Gita* is the scripture that is especially designed to guide the people of our age (the Kali Yuga). The central message of the *Gita* is that we are meant to live active and productive lives, gaining an education and having a career, becoming married and having children, while still living the life of a dedicated *yogi*. We are meant to operate within the world, but not be of the world, dedicating all of our seemingly mundane activities as humble offerings at the feet of Sriman Narayana.

"One achieves *bhakti* [devotional consciousness of God] by hearing and chanting about the Supreme Lord's special qualities, even while engaged in the ordinary activities of life in this world." (*Narada Bhakti Sutra*, 37)

"Therefore, without being attached to the fruits of activities, one should act as a matter of duty; for by working without attachment, one attains the Supreme." (*Bhagavad Gita*, 3.19)

"One can have no success in Yoga if one eats too much or eats too little. Nor can one be successful if one sleeps too much or does not sleep enough." (*Bhagavad Gita*, 6:16)

> Question: What are some practical ways in which we can incorporate meditation, *bhakti* (devotional consciousness) and an awareness of the Divine in our daily activities?

> Fact: Most members of Vedic societies lived very active and productive lives. The four traditional "Aims of Man", or *purusharthas*, are 1) Dharma (following Natural Law), 2) *artha* (seeking prosperity and success in the world), 3) *kama* (sattvic sensual enjoyment in the world), and finally 4) *moksha* (spiritual liberation). Thus, the Vedic goals consist of a balanced mixture of both spiritual and material aims.

11.1.2 Being a Dharma Activist

We know that we are living in a world that is currently experiencing multiple dire crises – social, economic, political, moral, cultural, philosophical and psychological. The root problem that our world is experiencing today, however, is primarily a spiritual one. The current spiritual crisis, which has in turn led to widespread depression, meaninglessness and hopelessness, is the source of every other problem that currently afflicts us in the world today. The best way to help the world with all its myriad problems is to address this root spiritual issue. We can all help our families, our communities and our world by being Dharma activists, even if only in our spare time. No matter how busy we have convinced ourselves that we are, we can all spare at least a few moments a day to help repair our suffering world.

198

"One who has no compassion for humanity in its suffering and does not sacrifice his impermanent body for the higher causes of religious principles or eternal glory is certainly pitied even by the immovable beings." (*Srimad Bhagavatam*, 6.10.8)

"It has been conclusively decided in the scriptures, after due consideration, that the ultimate goal for the welfare of human society is detachment from the bodily concept of life, and increased and steadfast attachment for the Supreme Lord, who is transcendental, beyond the modes of nature." (*Srimad Bhagavatam*, 4.22.21)

Guidance: There are many valid ways of expressing compassion toward others. When we see innocent people who are hungry or ill, we must give them food and assistance. We must have the ability to see both our own children and ourselves in the faces of those who are suffering around us. Simply helping people on the physical level alone, however, is only a short-term solution to alleviating their most immediate suffering. There are millions of well fed and comfortable people in America, for example, who are still tormented by immense inner sufferings, such as depression, a sense of meaninglessness, loneliness, etc. The most effective way to truly help people to alleviate their deeper suffering is to help them spiritually. So, when you meet a person who is suffering from such inner turmoil, give that person a copy of the *Bhagavad Gita* or of the book *Sanatana Dharma: The Eternal Natural Way* to help guide them, teach them patiently how to meditate and begin developing peace of mind, encourage them to begin pursuing life-transformative spiritual practices that will reintroduce joy into their lives. Once a person develops true internal strength from having a solid spiritual foundation, they will then have the ability to tackle their material problems by themselves!

11.1.3 Things You Can Do to Support Dharma

Followers of Sanatana Dharma believe in teaching, not preaching. We see it as one of our most important tasks to engage in non-fanatical and nonintrusive outreach to provide information about Dharma to sincere spiritual seekers. The movement known as the International Sanatana Dharma Society was created solely with this purpose in mind. In *Sanatana Dharma: The Eternal Natural Way*, we provide 20 different ways in which you can help in doing Dharma outreach. For the sake of this smaller study guide, we have narrowed these down to ten of the most important ways you can be a Dharma activist.

"Ashvins, Lords of Light, fill me with the sweetness of the honey-bee so I may speak of the glorious Word to the masses of people." (*Atharva Veda*, 6.69.2)

"Actual speech is that which describes the qualities of the Lord, real hands are those that work for Him, a true mind is that which always remembers Him dwelling within everything moving and nonmoving, and actual ears are those that listen to sanctifying topics about Him." (*Srimad Bhagavatam*, 10.80.3)

Exercise: Try your best to do as many of these activities as you possibly can to help support Dharma.

1. Distribute copies of "*Sanatana Dharma: The Eternal Natural Way*" and other ISDS publications to your friends, family and all sincere spiritual seekers you know. Give out these books as presents during the holidays and people's birthdays. Donate them to libraries, and recommend to bookstores that they carry our books.

2. Join the Sanatana Dharma Forum online discussion group that is found on Dharmacentral.com to feel more connected to our global online Vedic community. Learn and share ideas there for doing Dharma outreach.

3. Forward any of the many hundreds of Dharma memes that we have available in many different languages. These are available at Dharmacentral.com and on the Sanatana Dharma Forum.

4. Share the links to all of our inspiring and educational videos that are available at our YouTube channel: Youtube.com/dharmanation.

5. Print out and put up flyers about Sanatana Dharma on local bulletin boards in your city or neighborhood. Dharma flyers can be obtained at www.dharmacentral.com and on the Sanatana Dharma Forum.

6. Contact the International Sanatana Dharma Society to host a Dharma event in your community, your Yoga center, your university, or at your workplace.

7. Use music, art, stories, drama, film, and other creative media to explore themes of Dharma and spirituality.

8. Form or join a Dharma study group centered on *Sanatana Dharma: The Eternal Natural Way*, and other publications of the International Sanatana Dharma Society.

9. Become an active volunteer for your local branch of the International Sanatana Dharma Society, or on any of the many ISDS projects currently available. Information on such projects is available at either Dharmacentral.com or Sanatanadharma-forum.com.

10. Consider becoming a monthly tithing member of the International Sanatana Dharma Society.

Chapter 12 Resources

Here, we have presented a number of important Vedic resources to help deepen your understanding and practice of Dharma, including websites, periodicals and devotional supply stores. The greatest resource that you have at your disposal for exploring deeply the path of Vedic spirituality is the International Sanatana Dharma Society and the society's website Dharmacentral.com.

"In the association of pure devotees, discussion of the pastimes and activities of the Supreme Godhead is very pleasing and satisfying to the ear and the heart. By cultivating such knowledge one gradually becomes advanced on the path of liberation, and thereafter he is freed, and his attraction becomes fixed. Then real devotion and devotional service begin." (*Srimad Bhagavatam*, 3.25.25)

12.1.1 International Sanatana Dharma Society (ISDS)

The ISDS is the most authentically based organization dedicated to teaching Sanatana Dharma in the world today. This movement was created to help all sincere spiritual seekers to find the answers they are searching for, and to experience a global fellowship of spiritual practitioners in which they can be assured of spiritual growth under the excellent guidance of an exceedingly qualified *guru*.

"These are they who are conscious of the tremendous falsehood in the world; they grow in the house of Truth. They are the strong and invincible sons of Infinity." (*Rig Veda*, 7.60.5)

A Brief History of the International Sanatana Dharma Society

1985-1986
Having been a full-time Hindu monastic from 1978-1984, Sri Acharyaji started his own small, unofficial *ashrama* in his home in New York with several other former Hindu monastics.

1986
During a trip to India to be with his *guru*, Swami B.R. Shridhara, Acharyaji is requested by his *guru* to become an Acharya himself and to teach

Dharma to the world upon his return to America.

1988
Sri Acharyaji formally began teaching soon upon his arrival in the city of Chicago from New York. The first organization he founded was called the Yoga and Meditation Association (YAMA). Acharyaji led meditation gatherings at a local Yoga center under this organization's name.

1992
As an undergraduate student at Loyola University Chicago, Acharyaji began teaching Dharma on campus primarily to gatherings of students. He had changed the name of his organization to the Bhakti Vedanta Society (BVS), which consisted of a small board of directors, written by-laws, and a mission statement. Through the BVS, Acharyaji led a weekly *Bhagavad Gita* study group on campus, organized several *pujas*, and gave period talks on specific subjects.

1997
Soon after moving to Madison, Wisconsin to attend graduate school, Acharyaji founded a student organization on the University of Wisconsin-Madison campus called the Sanatana Dharma Students Association (SDSA). The SDSA had well-attended weekly meetings that included meditation, talks by Acharyaji, *puja*, and discussions. In addition, the SDSA would periodically organize much larger gatherings for important Hindu holidays and other special events.

1998
Realizing that the time was soon approaching when he would have to implement his *guru's* orders on a large scale, Acharyaji decided to begin the most formal of his organizational endeavors in the form of the International Sanatana Dharma Society. The ISDS was officially founded in 1998 in Madison, Wisconsin by Sri Dharma Pravartaka Acharya as an organizational vehicle to teach Dharma spirituality on the global stage. Dharmacentral.com was started at this same time as the online presence of the ISDS. From 1998 on, Acharyaji expanded his personal teaching activities dramatically - all while continuing to be a fulltime graduate student and father. He began conducting formal seminars on Yoga philosophy and spirituality at Main Street Yoga to audiences of 30-40 people. He also began traveling the nation giving talks on Dharma at academic conferences and Hindu temples.

2000

In 2000, Acharyaji begins offering six-week courses on the *Bhagavad Gita*, *Yoga Sutras*, and Sanskrit. The first four spiritual initiations took place this year with Acharyaji officiating as *guru*. In addition to leading weekly *satsanghas* in Madison, Acharyaji spends the next ten years traveling extensively on teaching tours.

2005

Acharyaji's two books, "*The Shakti Principle*" and "*The Art of Wisdom*", are released.

2007

After 10 years of conducting *satsanghas*, seminars and other events in Madison, Acharyaji moves to Omaha, Nebraska to become the Resident Acharya of the Hindu temple. All weekly *satsangha* activities now resumed in Omaha, in addition to a large offering of other classes and events.

2008

The ISDS is legally incorporated as a Nebraska state-recognized corporation. A local Board of Directors is established, in addition to a national Board of Trustees, and international Board of Advisors. "*Radical Universalism*" and "*Taking Refuge in Dharma*" books are released.

2009

The ISDS requests tax-exempt status from the IRS, which it receives three weeks later. A branch of the Sanatana Dharma Students Association (the student wing of the ISDS) is established at the University of Nebraska in Omaha. The ISDS now has many followers in Nebraska/Iowa, and thousands of supporters internationally. A committee of Hindu community leaders was established to procure a building to create a temple, *ashrama* and headquarters of the ISDS in Omaha.

2010

The ISDS temple building was bought and established in February, 2010 as the global headquarters of the ISDS. The ISDS temple is the second of only two Hindu temples in the state of Nebraska officially and legally recognized by the federal, state and county governments. The books, "*The Vedic Way of Knowing God*", "*Sanatana Dharma: The Eternal Natural Way*", and "*Living Dharma*" were all released.

2013

The Book "*The Dharma Manifesto*" is released.

2014

The ISDS establishes its second official branch in Austin, Texas. The ISDS YouTube channel (youtube.com/dharmanation) has 5000 subscribers. The book *"The Sanatana Dharma Study Guide"* is released.

2015

The ISDS expects to establish 2-3 new branches in America. There are plans to release several more books this year, including *"The Encyclopedia of Sanatana Dharma"*, *"Vedanta: The Culmination of Wisdom"*, *"The Dharma Dialogues"*, *"Isha Upanishad"* (translation and commentary), and *"Bhagavad Gita"* (translation and commentary). We will also be venturing into the creation of many large-scale multimedia projects, including documentaries, audio CD production and professional podcasting. 2015 is expected to be the most successful year of growth that the ISDS has ever experienced. The ISDS Youtube channel now has over 6400 members.

"In each and every age *satsangha* is the supreme means of liberation." (*Uddhava Gita*, 7:5)

12.1.2 Distinctly Authentic Approach to Vedic Spirituality

There is no other Vedic movement that is doing more to teach authentic Sanatana Dharma in the world today than the ISDS. There are many qualities that make the ISDS movement unique. These include:

1) A strict adherence to the Guru Principle (*guru tattva*) and the importance of disciplic succession (*parampara*) and spiritual lineage (*sampradaya*).

2) Everything that the ISDS teaches and practices is scripturally based. As can be seen from the multiple Vedic verses cited throughout this book, we make sure that everything we teach and do can be traced back directly to the Vedic scriptures, and/or to previous authorized Acharyas. The ISDS is the purest organizational manifestation of the teachings of the Vedic scriptures.

3) We insist on academic excellence in support of Vedic philosophy. While it is not at all necessary that a person be a scholar or

philosopher in order to be a supporter of the ISDS, we do maintain very high academic standards in everything we publish or re-release. We also maintain close working ties with many of the world's leading academic authorities on the Vedic tradition.

4) Quality over quantity is one of our most important mottos. While we certainly do engage in outreach with the goal of having the ISDS continue in its global growth, the emphasis of the ISDS will always be upon the quality of our teachings, practices, leadership, and the people who we allow to become members.

5) Vedic Authenticity: We are neither a New Age nor a syncretist path. We do not mix and match Vedic spirituality with other popular or fad forms of spirituality, or with other religious paths. Our religion is exclusively Sanatana Dharma. Everything we do and teach is purely Vedic in origin and content.

6) The ISDS is the most comprehensive Vedic movement in the world today. The goal of our movement is to bring about a total spiritual restoration upon the Earth. This means affecting the world on every level of interaction, including cultural, scientific, economic, and social, in addition to spiritual.

7) The ISDS teaches the most effective *sadhana* available today. Each and all of the *sadhana* techniques taught by the ISDS are directly sourced to the Vedic and Yoga literature, and have been taught in an unbroken lineage (*sampradaya*) stretching back historically to God. In addition, several of the *sadhana* techniques taught by the ISDS are practices that have been neglected for many centuries due to the esoteric nature of the techniques, and the inaccessibility of the Vedic texts in which they are found. The ISDS couples philosophical accuracy with a deep emphasis on effective and authentic practice.

8) The ISDS upholds the highest ethical standards of any Vedic spirituality movement on the Earth today. Every leader, manager, priest and teacher of the ISDS is expected to fully adhere to the strictest moral and ethical standards outlined in the Vedic scriptures. Any leader who does not meet the highest ethical standards is required to immediately relinquish his or her post in the ISDS.

"Strive, strive only for the association of pure devotees of Lord Krishna."
(*Narada Bhakti Sutras*, 42)

12.1.3 Becoming a Member of the ISDS

There are two formal requirements for becoming a member of the ISDS.

1. You must consider Sanatana Dharma to be your spiritual tradition.

2. All members are expected to tithe monthly in accordance with their means.

"Simply by detachment from the association of worldly people, and by associating with exalted devotees, anyone can attain perfection of knowledge and with the sword of knowledge can cut to pieces the illusory associations within this material world. Through the association of devotees, one can engage in the service of the Lord by hearing and chanting. Thus one can revive his dormant God consciousness and, sticking to the cultivation of God consciousness, return home, back to Godhead, even in this life." (*Srimad Bhagavatam*, 5.12.16)

12.1.4 Books by Sri Dharma Pravartaka Acharya

The following is a list of authoritative books that we would recommend for accurate and detailed information about Sanatana Dharma.

Sanatana Dharma: The Eternal Natural Way

The Sanatana Dharma Study Guide

The Encyclopedia of Sanatana Dharma

The Vedic Way of Knowing God

Living Dharma: The Teachings of Sri Dharma Pravartaka Acharya

Radical Universalism: Are All Religions the Same?

The Dharma Manifesto: A New Vision for Global Transformation

The Dharma Dialogues

Vedanta: The Culmination of Wisdom

Taking Refuge in Dharma: The Initiation Guidebook

The Shakti Principle: Encountering the Feminine Power of God

The Art of Wisdom: Affirmations for Boundless Living

Books by A.C. Bhaktivedanta Swami Prabhupada

Bhagavad-Gita As It Is

Krsna: The Supreme Personality of Godhead

The Nectar of Devotion: The Complete Science of Bhakti Yoga

The Perfection of Yoga

Sri Isopanisad

Easy Journey to Other Planets

The Science of Self-Realization

Raja-vidya: The King of Knowledge

Books by Dr. David Frawley

From the River of Heaven: Vedic Knowledge for the Modern Age

Awaken Bharata: A Call for India's Rebirth

How I Became a Hindu: My Discovery of Vedic Dharma

Yoga, the Greater Tradition

Vedantic Meditation: Lighting the Flame of Awareness

Beyond the Mind

Yoga and the Sacred Fire: Self-realization and Planetary Transformation

Ayurveda and the Mind: The Healing of Consciousness

Gods, Sages and Kings: Vedic Secrets of Ancient Civilization

Books by Stephen Knapp

Proof of Vedic Culture's Global Existence

The Power of the Dharma: An Introduction to Hinduism and Vedic Culture

Yoga and Meditation: Their Real Purpose and How to Get Started

Avatars, Gods and Goddesses of Vedic Culture

The Soul: Understanding Our Real Identity

How the Universe was Created and Our Purpose In It

Periodicals

Hinduism Today Magazine

Dharma Websites

www.dharmacentral.com

www.youtube.com/DharmaNation

www.sanatanadharmaforum.com

www.vedanet.com

Quizzes

You can either take these quizzes by yourself, with your family, or in a
Sanatana Dharma study group. Have fun with them, and let them insti-
gate interesting discussions. Not all the answers to these quizzes are
found in this book – but are dependent upon an understanding of Vedic
spirituality more generally. The answers are revealed at the end of the
Quiz section.

210

Quiz 1

1. Two major epics of Sanatana Dharma are the *Ramayana* and the *Maha-bharata*:   True or False

2. Valmiki is the author of the epic *Ramayana*:   True or False

3. The *Bhagavad Gita* was written 500 years after the Qur'an:
                                                          True or False

4. The *Ramayana* takes place during the cosmic age known as the Treta Yuga: True or False

5. Lord Krishna is the Hindu god of playfulness and love: True or False

6. The *Upanishads* teach us to eat, drink and be merry: True or False

7. Sri Rama was born in the city of Ayodhya: True or False

8. Sri Krishna was born in Vrindavan: True or False

9. Dharmis believe in many gods, and not only one God: True or False

10. Dharmis worship idols: True or False

11. Sanatana Dharma is the most important and relevant religion in the world today: True or False

Answer these questions:

What does it mean to be compassionate?

What are some of the special features of Sanatana Dharma?

Quiz 2

1. The term "*Bhagavad Gita*" means "Teachings to Arjuna":

True or False

2. Sri Laksmi is the Goddess of Growth: True or False

3. Dharmis are vegetarian because we're afraid the animals we eat might have been our deceased grandmother: True or False

4. Yoga is a school of Vedic philosophy: True or False

5. More people practice Yoga in the West than India: True or False

6. Sanatana Dharma teaches us that ultimately nothing is of importance:

True or False

7. In the *Bhagavad Gita*, Lord Krishna tries to convince Arjuna that he shouldn't fight the Mahabharata War, and should instead live a life of complete non-violence: True or False

8. Gandhi was a very important Vedic religious leader: True or False

9. Lord Krishna's final teachings to Arjuna in the *Bhagavad Gita* is that the soul doesn't really exist anyway, so he might as well fight:

True or False

10. Sanatana Dharma teaches us to be strong, fearless, and assertive:

True or False

11. "Hinduism" is not the real name of our religion: True or False

How Do You Respond?

> "You Hindus are idol worshipers with so many gods. We Christians have a better religion because we believe in only one God, and that Jesus has saved us with his sacrifice on the cross. Why don't you just become Christian?"

212

Quiz 3

1. The *Upanishads* are ceremonial scriptures with rules for conducing Vedic fire rituals: True or False

2. You need to be vegetarian to be Hindu: True or False

3. You can only be Hindu if you're born Hindu: True or False

4. The fastest growing religion in Lithuania and Russia is Sanatana Dharma: True or False

5. There are 5 million Hindus in America: True or False

6. The main focus of Yoga is meditation: True or False

7. The highest concept in Sanatana Dharma is the Trimurti: True or False

8. You can only practice Sanatana Dharma fully and 100% if you're a *yogi*, a *swami*, or a *sadhu*:   True or False

9. The idea of caste is one of the cornerstones of Sanatana Dharma: True or False

10. Lord Krishna's highest instruction to Arjuna is to renounce the entire world and become a *sannyasi*:   True or False

11. Lord Krishna's highest instruction to Arjuna is to follow his caste duties: True or False

12. Lord Krishna tells Arjuna to abandon all lesser *dharmas*:   True or False

13. Bollywood movies are a reflection of Vedic culture: True or False

14. There are more people practicing Ayurveda in America and Europe than in India at present: True or False

15. India is a Hindu Nation: True or False

16. The word "VEDA" means "The Hindu Scripture":   True or False

17. Sanatana Dharma teaches that it will take millions of years to become liberated: True or False

18. Sanatana Dharma teaches that everything is God: True or False

19. Ancient Vedic people would never allow their photos to be taken for fear that it would give them bad *karma*:   True or False

20. The Martial Arts were created as a Vedic art: True or False

What's Wrong with this Sentence?

> "Hindus worship idols of cows and their religion teaches that being strong, courageous and assertive is being too materialistic. Instead, they teach that we should all pray to a fearful God in a cave for most of our time"

Quiz 4

1. Lord Krishna's city of Dvaraka sank into the sea: True or False

2. The principle of *ahimsa* teaches us to turn the other cheek and accept defeat if we are attacked: True or False

3. Lord Ganapati has a missing tusk because he broke it off to write a book: True or False

4. The Ganga River partially travels through space along its route:
      True or False

5. The word "*mantra*" means "repeated sound":   True or False

6. Surya is the supreme being of Sanatana Dharma: True or False

7. Socrates and Plato were followers of Dharma: True or False

8. Rama was a mortal king: True or False

9. Most of the world was Vedic 5000 years ago: True or False

10. Sanatana Dharma teaches that Truth is relative: True or False

11. The three Tattvas are three types of philosophy: True or False

Discussion:

What is my experience at school and/or work as a follower of Sanatana Dharma?

Quiz 5

1. The three *gunas* are three different ways that Krishna dances with Radha: True or False

2. To create things is to act in *sattva guna*:   True or False

3. We can be good followers of Sanatana Dharma and still listen to Classical music or Rock: True or False

4. We can be good followers of Sanatana Dharma and still listen to "Gangsta' Rap" and "Black Metal":   True or False

5. Lord Shiva preserves reality until he finally destroys it: True or False

6. The mantra Aum Namo Narayanaya means "Oh Lord Narayana, please give me Your blessings."   True or False

7. Sanatana Dharma teaches us that the body is bad and the soul is good: True or False

8. Jerusalem is the most sacred land in the world: True or False

9. I should be "Hindu" just because my parents are "Hindu":
                                                              True or False

10. Tens of millions of Americans and Europeans will become followers of Sanatana Dharma in my lifetime: True or False

Answer this question:

What does Sanatana Dharma mean to me?

216

Quiz 6

1. There were flying vehicles during the Vedic era (over 5,000 years ago):
                                                    True or False

2. Any genuine teacher should be considered a *guru* – a sitar teacher, a dance teacher, even a math teacher: True or False

3. The sole goal of Yoga is to make us physically fit: True or False

4. The *Vedas* say we shouldn't eat chocolate: True or False

5. It's not good to be too surrendered to God: True or False

6. Hanuman is currently living in the Himalayas: True or False

7. The word *santosha* means "without pride":   True or False

8. Sanatana Dharma teaches us to be good in thought, word and deed:
                                                    True or False

9. To be humble means not to be too forceful in standing up for the Truth: True or False

10. The highest teaching of Sanatana Dharma is that "we're all one":
                                                    True or False

11. Does Sanatana Dharma teache that we have a soul, or that we are a soul?   (a) We have a soul.   (b) We are a soul.

Complete the following sentence with as much detail as time affords:

       "God is…"

Question: How can we reflect God's qualities in our own lives?

Quiz 7

1. Brahman is the highest philosophical term for God in Sanatana Dharma: True or False

2. Latin and Greek originated from Sanskrit: True or False

3. Vedic warriors are taught to muster up as much anger as possible before having a battle: True or False

4. Women cannot become religious leaders, like *swamis, gurus, sadhus*, etc., in Sanatana Dharma: True or False

5. Sarasvati is the Goddess of Civilization: True or False

6. Lord Vekateshvara is an incarnation of Shiva: True or False

7. Lord Shiva destroys the universe by sitting deeply still in meditation and willing it: True or False

8. In meditation, the goal is to make our minds blank: True or False

9. A *guru, swami* or *acharya* carries a staff with him to hit people on the head when they get in his way: True or False

What's Wrong with this Sentence?

> "The culture of Sanatana Dharma can be described in four words: caste, cows, curry, and cobras."

Questions:

> "What makes me happy?"

> "Who do I admire most in life?"

> "What is the goal for my life?"

Quiz 8

1. Brahma, Brahman, and brahmin all mean the same thing:
$$\text{True or False}$$

2. Vedic people wear *kunkum* (a red dot) on their foreheads to mark the third eye: True or False

3. We take our shoes off before entering the temple to signify that we're stepping on pure and sacred ground: True or False

4. The word "Hindu" means "noble one": True or False

5. The word "*arya*" means Scandinavian: True or False

6. Ganapati has an elephant's head in order to show how humorous God can be: True or False

7. There are one billion followers of Sanatana Dharmia in the world:
$$\text{True or False}$$

8. Sanatana Dharma teaches that all religions are the same: True or False

9. Sanatana Dharma accepts the Old Testament and the Qur'an as authoritative scriptures: True or False

10. Yahweh, Allah and Narayana are all the same being: True or False

Answer the following:

"What brought me to Sanatana Dharma?"

Discussion:

How do you discuss Sanatana Dharma with your children or with kids who aren't very religious?

Quiz 9

1. George Harrison of the Beatles was a Dharmi: True or False

2. Julia Roberts is a Dharmi: True or False

3. Richard Gere is a follower of Sanatana Dharma: True or False

4. Lord Krishna says in the *Bhagavad Gita* that we should meditate on Him and think of Him: True or False

5. India is presently a Dharma Nation: True or False

6. Mount Kailasha in the Himalayas is sacred to followers of Sanatana Dharma, Buddhism, Jainism and the Bon religion: True or False

7. Sanskrit is not a spoken language any more: True or False

8. The fastest growing religion in Indonesia today is Sanatana Dharma:
         True or False

9. The original religion of Indonesia before Islam conquered them was Sanatana Dharma: True or False

10. Maharishi Unviersity of Management is a major university in Fairfield, Iowa with almost a thousand students studying Vedic sciences:
         True or False

11. There was a Dharma-based political party that came in fifth place in the U.S. Presidential race in 2000:   True or False

Discussion:

It is correct to say "God is truth", but it is incorrect to say that "Truth is God". Why?

What's wrong with this statement?:

"All religions lead to the same place, just like all roads lead to the top of the mountain. So, it doesn't matter which religion you practice, since they're all the same anyway."

220

Quiz 10

1. The largest Vedic temple in the world is in Tamil Nadu: True or False

2. The largest Vedic temple in the world is Angkor Wat in Cambodia:
True or False

3. The national airline of Indonesia is called "Garuda Airlines":
True or False

4. Archeologists have found *murtis* of Vishnu in Russia dating from the 10th century: True or False

5. The word "Ireland" means "Land of the Aryas": True or False

6. The Danaan, or Mycenean, or Doric civilization who dominated ancient Greece from 1500 BCE were Vedic warriors to settled in Greece from Aryavarta: True or False

7. God is a human: True or False

8. God is a person: True or False

9. Vishnu and Shiva don't get along: True or False

10. The *devas* (gods) and *devis* (goddesses) are all just different forms of God. It doesn't matter which one you worship. Just pick any one!
True or False

11. Pre-Christian European religions are offshoots of Sanatana Dharma:
True or False

Discussion:

"How do I practice Sanatana Dharma in my own life?"

Quiz 11

1. Hanuman is the god of monkeys: True or False

2. It is auspicious to offer a prayer to Sarasvati before starting school and before tests: True or False

3. The ideas in the *Bhagavad Gita* were inspired by the teachings of Christianity: True or False

4. If I become a more spiritual person, that means that I need to give up the pleasures of life: True or False

5. Only Sanatana Dharma teaches reincarnation: True or False

6. Only Sanatana Dharma has the practice of image worship: True or False

7. To be proud of Sanatana Dharma is false ego: True or False

8. Even though he fought on the wrong side in the battle of Kurukshetra, Bhishma was a great devotee of Lord Krishna: True or False

9. Dharmis have a shrine to "the Unknown God" in every temple: True or False

10. Lord Krsna says in the *Bhagavad Gita*: "Oh Arjuna, I declare unto you that if someone hits you on one cheek, turn and offer him the other." True or False

11. Sanatana Dharma teaches that pious women should have their head covered by their sari in public: True or False

12. The Buddha was a follower of Sanatana Dharma for the full duration of his life: True or False

What's Wrong with this Sentence?

"Sanatana Dharma does not believe in others joining our religion. If you were born Christian, Muslim, Buddhist, or whatever, you should just stay in that religion."

Quiz 12

1. Sanatana Dharma teaches that God is completely transcendent and not in the world: True or False

2. Bhishma, the grandfather of the Pandavas, had the power to choose the time of his death: True or False

3. Chanakya was a Vedic priest who was responsible for ridding India of Greek invaders: True or False

4. The three highest goddesses are Pushpadevi, Narakadevi, and Bandhadevi: True or False

5. Chanakya wrote two books: the *Artha Shastra* and the *Chanakya Purana*:
                                                                True or False

6. Subhash Chandra Bose was a follower of Gandhi and fought to free India non-violently: True or False

7. *Kundalini* is a powerful energy that lies coiled at the bottom of the spine: True or False

8. The two saints, Andal and Mirabai, both symbolically married Krishna:
                                                                True or False

9. Sarasvati holds a vina instrument because she is the goddess of arts:
                                                                True or False

10. The *devas* and *devis* eventually die and are reborn according to their *karma*:   True or False

What's Wrong with this Sentence?

> "The myth of Krishna is an amusing story"

Quiz 13

1. The three *ashvagandha* trees liberated by Lord Shiva were actually very great devotees: True or False

2. The Ganga river originates from the hair of Lord Shiva: True or False

3. Ganapati has a broken tusk because he lost it in the great battle of Kurukshetra: True or False

4. The two most important symbols of Lord Narayana are the *chakra* (wheel) and the *shankha* (conchshell): True or False

5. Following the principle of *ahimsa*, Lord Rama never killed another living being, even though He was a warrior: True or False

6. The highest goal of Sanatana Dharma is to always create good *karma*, and never bad *karma*: True or False

7. The gods, like Surya, Indra, and Chandra, are immortal: True or False

8. The *Bhagavad Gita* teaches that we should abandon all *dharmas* and simply surrender to Lord Krishna: True or False

What's wrong with this sentence?

"The Indian religion believes in caste, fate, idols, otherworldliness, and poverty."

Questions:

How do I explain what Sanatana Dharma is to others?
How do I know that Sanatana Dharma is the right religion for me?
What sorts of spiritual things do I do when I visit the temple?

Quiz 14

1. Once you become a *yogi*, you need to quit your job: True or False

2. We are taught to fear God in Sanatana Dharma: True or False

3. Sanatana Dharma encourages us to nurture inner strength, courage, fearlessness and determination: True or False

4. It doesn't matter which god or goddess you worship. They're all the same anyway: True or False

5. Krishna encouraged Arjuna to fight for justice, not to denounce his duty: True or False

6. Sanatana Dharma is a polytheistic religion: True or False

7. The principle of Sri Guru is foundational to Sanatana Dharma and to any serious form of spirituality: True or False

8. Sanatana Dharma teaches that each person has his own truth and that there is no one, higher Truth: True or False

9. The pre-Christian European religions are all offshoots of the much earlier Vedic religion: True or False

Discussion:

"What am I searching for on my spiritual journey?"

Quiz 15

1. Lakshmi Devi is responsible for growth in nature: True or False

2. There are temples in India where there is human sacrifice to Kali:
     True or False

3. Lord Shiva is called Nilakanta because he drank an ocean of poison that turned his throat blue: True or False

4. Krishnaloka is the birthplace of Lord Krishna: True or False

5. A *chakra* is an energy system in the psychic body, and a weapon of Lord Narayana: True or False

6. It is necessary to be celebate to be a *guru*:   True or False

7. The Gopis of Vrindavana are considered to be the highest example of *bhakti*:   True or False

8. Parvati is the same as "Mother Nature":   True or False

9. Dharmis believe that the universe is God: True or False

Question:

Why are Narayana, Shiva, and Devi the most worshiped beings in Sanatana Dharma?

What's wrong with these sentences?

"Sanatana Dharma teaches that all religions are the same."

"The Eastern religion of Sanatana Dharma is a universal religions for all Asians."

226

Quiz 16

1. Lord Rama is the last *avatara* of God, and appeared about 5100 years ago: True or False

2. Many of the founders of the Straight Edge rock movement were followers of Sanatana Dharma: True or False

3. There are three realm in the universe; a) heavenly, b) earthly, and c) hellish: True or False

4. The principle of reincarnation teaches that with every incarnation, we are in higher and higher bodies: True or False

5. The name of the text *"Brahma Sutras"* can be translated as "The Creation Story of the god Brahma":   True or False

6. Worshiping the Buddha is an acceptable practice in Sanatana Dharma:
                                                                               True or False

7. While Sanatana Dharma rejects the theology of mainstream Christianity, we accept Jesus himself as a great *guru*:   True or False

8. Many of the early Greek and Roman philosophers were either influenced directly by Dharmic thought, or at least taught similar ideas. (For example, Apollonius, Ammonius Saccus, Plotinus.):   True or False

9. Krishna, Govinda, Gopala, Gopinatha and Madhusudana are all different names for the same person: True or False

Question:

What is the best way to practice Sanatana Dharma today?

How Do You Respond?

"You Dharmis are idol worshipers with so many gods. We Muslims have a better religion because we believe in only one God, and that Islam is the one true faith. Why don't you just become Muslim?"

Quiz 17

1. *Karma* is a doctrine of free-choice, and not of fate: True or False

2. Worshiping images in not the norm among most religions:
                                                    True or False

3. The Battle of Kurukshetra has been proven to be a true story:
                                                    True or False

4. The reason why *avataras* appear is to uphold *karma* and to fight *akarma*:
                                                    True or False

5. Narasimha-avatara was half man and half lion: True or False

6. Only arranged marriages are accepted in Sanatana Dharma:
                                                    True or False

7. Arjuna gave up the chance to have all of Lord Krishna's armies fight on his side in the Battle of Kurukshetra: True or False

8. While it is not necessary to be a vegetarian to simply be a follower of Sanatana Dharma, vegetarianism is necessary if one wants to make spiritual progress in Sanatana Dharma: True or False

What's Wrong with this Sentence?

"The idol of the Indian god Vekateshvara was first established in Tirupati 4000 years ago to commemorate the myth of Lord Krishna."

Question:

Why is having a *guru* indispensible in spiritual practice?

228

Quiz 18

1. Abraham (the originator of Judaism, Christianity and Islam) was born in a Vedic city: True or False

2. The Celtic people of ancient Europe had their own *Vedas*:
True or False

3. The degeneration of modern society was foretold in the *Mahabharata* 5000 years ago: True or False

4. Sri Lakshmi is the co-eternal Absolute along with Sriman Narayana:
True or False

5. The Nagas are a race of reptilians: True or False

6. The Buddha converted the Naga race to Dharma: True or False

7. The present Indian state of Nagaland is the original homeland of the Naga serpents: True or False

8. In traditional Vedic religion, women have to walk three steps behind their husbands, keep their heads covered, and are not allowed to be in any leadership position: True or False

9. The *Rig Veda* is the oldest writing in all of world literature:
True or False

10. The term "Aum Tat Sat" means "ow, I sat on a tack": True or False

11. Buddhism worships the same *devas* as Sanatana Dharma does:
True or False

12. Sanatana Dharma teaches that very ugly species (like mosquitoes) don't have souls: True or False

Discussion:

"What can I do to very practically support Dharma today?"

Quiz 19

1. Ancient statues of Vedic *devas* have been found throughout much of Asia and Europe: True or False

2. There are only two Vedic temples dedicated to Ganapati in the U.S.:   True or False

3. There are ten major incarnations of Shiva who come to uphold Dharma: True or False

4. The Celtic people of ancient Europe had their own *brahmana* priests, known as the Druids: True or False

5. You can only be a follower of Sanatana Dharma if you were born into the religion: True or False

6. All vegetarians are Hindus and all Hindus are vegetarians: True or False

7. There are about 23 million vegetarians in the U.S.:   True or False

8. In Sanatana Dharma, women are allowed to be in any leadership position within the religion: True or False

9. Sanatana Dharma is the most ancient religion known to the world: True or False

10. Sanatana Dharma teaches that non-humans don't have souls: True or False

What's Wrong with this Sentence?

"When animal sacrifices to Vishnu were finally stopped in Hinduism around the time of Shiva, the common people, who weren't very philosophical, then turned to bhakti out of a fear of angering God."

230

Quiz 20

1. We should see the *guru* as our pal and colleague: True or False

2. Humility is the same as humiliation: True or False

3. The *rishis* were all celibate monks: True or False

4. We use a *mala* for *japa* meditation in order to keep track of the number of *mantras* and to help concentrate: True or False

5. When possible, it is helpful and inspiring to sit and meditate in front of the *murti* in the temple: True or False

6. When we need help, it is wrong to bother God with our prayers:
True or False

7. Sanatana Dharma and Buddhism are pretty much the same path:
True or False

What is wrong with this sentence?

"The idol of Lord Ganapati is based on a beautiful myth from the Indian scriptures."

Questions:

Why is God important to me?

Is doing good the same as being good?

Why did Krishna want Arjuna to fight in the Mahabharata War?

Quiz Answer Key

Quiz 1: 1=T, 2=T, 3=F, 4=T, 5=F, 6=F, 7=T, 8=F, 9=F, 10=F, 11=T

Quiz 2: 1=F, 2=T, 3=F, 4=T, 5=T, 6=F, 7=F, 8=F, 9=F, 10=T, 11=T

Quiz 3: 1–F, 2–F, 3=F, 4=T, 5=T, 6=T, 7=F, 8=F, 9=F, 10=F, 11=F, 12=T, 13=F, 14=T, 15=F, 16=F, 17=F, 18=F, 19=F, 20=T

Quiz 4: 1=T, 2=F, 3=T, 4=T, 5=F, 6=F, 7=T, 8=F, 9=T, 10=F, 11=F

Quiz 5: 1=F, 2=F, 3=T, 4=F, 5=F, 6=F, 7=F, 8=F, 9=F, 10=T

Quiz 6: 1=T, 2=T, 3=F, 4=F, 5=F, 6=T, 7=F, 8=T, 9=F, 10=F, 11=B

Quiz 7: 1=T, 2=T, 3=F, 4=F, 5=T, 6=F, 7=F, 8=F, 9=F

Quiz 8: 1=F, 2=T, 3=T, 4=F, 5=F, 6=F, 7=T, 8=F, 9=F, 10=F

Quiz 9: 1=T, 2=T, 3=F, 4=T, 5=F, 6=T, 7=F, 8=T, 9=T, 10=T, 11=T

Quiz 10: 1=F, 2=T, 3=T, 4=T, 5=T, 6=T, 7=F, 8=T, 9=F, 10=F, 11=F

Quiz 11: 1=F, 2=T, 3=F, 4=F, 5=F, 6=F, 7=F, 8=T, 9=F, 10=F, 11=F, 12=T

Quiz 12: 1=F, 2=T, 3=T, 4=F, 5=F, 6=F, 7=T, 8=T, 9=T, 10=T

Quiz 13: 1=T, 2=F, 3=F, 4=T, 5=F, 6=F, 7=F, 8=T

Quiz 14: 1=F, 2=F, 3=T, 4=F, 5=T, 6=F, 7=T, 8=F, 9=T

Quiz 15: 1=T, 2=F, 3=T, 4=F, 5=T, 6=F, 7=T, 8=T, 9=F

Quiz 16: 1=F, 2=T, 3=T, 4=F, 5=F, 6=T, 7=T, 8=T, 9=T

Quiz 17: 1=T, 2=F, 3=T, 4=F, 5=T, 6=F, 7=T, 8=T

Quiz 18: 1=T, 2=T, 3=T, 4=T, 5=T, 6=T, 7=F, 8=F, 9=T, 10=F, 11=T, 12=F

Quiz 19: 1=T, 2=T, 3=F, 4=T, 5=F, 6=F, 7=T, 8=T, 9=T, 10=F

Quiz 20: 1=F, 2=F, 3=F, 4=T, 5=T, 6=F, 7=F

Sanatana Dharma by the Numbers

Three Gunas: *sattva / rajas / tamas*

Three Kandas: *karma-kanda / jnana-kanda / upasana-kanda*

Three Margas: Vaishnava / Shaiva / Shakta

Three Material Challenges (Tapa-traya): (1) Challenges arising from the mind and body, (2) challenges inflicted by other living beings, and (3) challenges arising from natural catastrophes over which one has no control.

Three Planetary Systems: Svarga (upper) / Bhu (middle) / Patala (lower)

Three Pramanas: *pratyaksha / anumana / shabda*

Three Tattvas: Atman / Brahman / Jagat

Three Truth Verifiers: Shastra / Acharya / Vichara

Three Vimas: The three dimensions.

Four Sampradayas: Śri / Brahma / Rudra / Kumara

Four Vedas: *Rig / Sama / Atharva / Yajur*

Seven Mothers: The biological mother, the wife of a *guru*, the wife of a king, the wife of a *brahmana*, the cow, the nurse, and Mother Earth.

Seven Physical Layers: skin, flesh, blood, marrow, bone, fat and semen.

Number of Species in the Material World: 8,400,000

Number of Human Species: 400,000

Duration of the Kali Yuga: 432,000 years

Glossary

Abhaya:	Fearlessness.
Abhyasa:	Practice.
Acharya:	Spiritual Preceptor. *Guru*. Representative of a spiritual lineage.
Acharya-asana:	Seat of the Acharya.
Agni:	The Vedic god of the altar fire who mediates between the gods and humans. He is first mentioned in the *Rig Veda*.
Ahamkara:	The artificial and illusory sense of self, lit. "I-maker."
Aham Pratyaya:	I-Cognition. The healthy sense of "I" as distinct from others.
Ahimsa:	Non-violence, including vegetarianism.
Ajna Chakra:	Spiritual centre between the eyebrows.
Ajñana:	Ignorance. Non-knowledge.
Akasha:	Ether.
Anahata Chakra:	Energy center located at the heart region.
Ananda:	Bliss, happiness, enjoyment.
Anitya:	Non-eternal, temporal, fleeting, transient. The ever-changing nature of experience.
Anga:	Body, limb, member.
Antahkarana:	The fourfold internal organs: Manas, Chitta, Buddhi and Ahamkara.

Anubhava: Experience.

Aparigraha: Non-possession, one of the five *yamas* (absti nences) of *ashtanga-yoga*.

Apavarga: Liberation, emancipation. Synonymous with *moksha*.

Apunya: Absence of merit, evil, non-virtuous. The oppo site of *punya*.

Artha: Aim, purpose, goal, meaning.

Asana: The physical poses of the Yoga system.

Ashrama: A retreat, hermitage, or secluded place where the principles of Yoga and meditation are prac ticed.

Ashuddhi: Impure, sullied.

Asteya: Non-stealing, non-theft, one of the five *yamas* (abstinences) of *ashtanga-yoga*.

Atman: The true, eternal, and essential self.

AUM: Divine sound representing the omni-presence of God. The primordial sound out of which all other sounds are born.

Avatara: A Divine descent of God into the earthly ma nifestation. *Avataras* of God come to earth to uphold Dharma and to battle *adharma*.

Avidya: Ignorance.

Bhagavad Gita: The Song of God. The primary scripture of Sanatana Dharma.

Bhakti: Devotional consciousness.

Brahmachari: Celibate student.

Brahmacharya: Sexual restraint, one of the five *yamas* (absti nences) of *ashtanga-yoga*.

Buddha: Awakened. The *avesha-avatara* of God seen as the "founder" of Buddhism.

Buddhi: Wisdom Faculty, intellect, understanding.

Chaitanya: Consciousness.

Chakra: Wheel, circle. Symbol of Dharma. One of sev en psychic energy centers in the subtle body.

Chit: Knowledge.

Chitta: Mind-substance, reason, intelligence.

Chitta-vritti: Activity of mind, thought, fluctuations of the mind.

Chitta-vritti-nirodha: Restraint or restriction of fluctuations of the mind. The first definition of Yoga given by Pa tañjali in his *Yoga Sutras* (1:2).

Chetana: Mind, understanding, sense.

Dana: Charity.

Darshana: View, perspective, observation, seeing. The phi losophical systems of Sanatana Dharma are known as Darshanas. They all recognize the insights of the *Vedas* as their foundation. Dar shana also means to view a sacred image or to have the audience of a sage.

Dakshina: Gift in gratitude to the spiritual teacher.

Deha: Physical body.

Desha: Place, locus, nation.

Deva/Devi: Lesser gods/goddesses of Sanatana Dharma. Similar to angels.

Dharana:	Concentration, the sixth of the eight limbs of Yoga.
Dharma:	Natural Law/Way. Intrinsic principles of cosmic operation.
Dharmi:	A follower of Sanatana Dharma.
Dhyana:	Meditation, the seventh of the eight limbs of Yoga
Diksha:	Spiritual initiation by a qualified *guru*.
Duhkha:	Dissatisfaction, pain, sorrow, frustration.
Drashtr:	The seer, experiencer, consciousness, *atman*.
Drashtuh-svarupa:	The true, spiritual form of the experiencer, or consciousness. That which is known when thought is stilled.
Drishti:	Drishti is the focus of the eyes in meditation in which one attempts to attain concentration alignment, and inner and outer balance. One actually does this to prevent distractions, but should be looking inwardly and not concentrate on the physical object. The object of focus could be the tip of your nose, in between your eyebrows, or a sacred image (*murti*) of the Divine.
Grihasta:	Householder.
Guna:	The three constituents of prime matter, which are: *sattva* (lightness, radiance or illumination), *rajas* (activity or passion), *tamas*. (darkness, heaviness or inertia).
Guru:	Teacher. Spiritual mentor and guide.
Hare Rama Mantra:	Hare Rama Hare Rama Rama Rama Hare Hare /

Hare Krishna Hare Krishna
Krishna Krishna Hare Hare.

Hiranyagarbha: The founder of Yoga; the first cosmological principle to emerge out of the infinite Reality; also called Brahma.

Indrĭya: The sense organs.

Ishvara: Master, lord, or king. Another term for God. Narayana.

Ishvara-pranidhana: Devotion to Ishvara, selfless action, one of the five *niyamas* (observances) of Yoga.

Jada: Insentient, lifeless.

Japa: Repetition of a *mantra*.

Japa-mala: A sting of 108 beads used for *mantra* meditation.

Jaya: Mastery, conquering, being victorious.

Jivatma: The individual self, a living individual.

Jñana: Wisdom, knowledge, understanding.

Kali-yuga: The present historical cyclic era. The Age of Conflict.

Kama: Passion, desire, lust, sensory enjoyment.

Karma: "Action". The principle that for every ethical action, there is a reaction.

Karuna: Compassion toward all sentient beings.

Kala: Time.

Kaivalya: Isolation, aloneness, single, unitary, uncompounded. Synonymous with *moksha*, or spiritual liberation.

240

Kapila:	The sage who originated Samkhya philosophy.
Klesha:	Affliction, pain, distress. According to Patañjali there are five *kleshas*: 1) *avidya* (ignorance), 2) *asmita* (I-am-ness, the artificial sense of self), 3) *raga* (attraction), 4) *dvesha* (aversion), and 5) *abhinivesha* (clinging to life). He also outlines four states the *kleshas* exist in: a) *prasupta* (dormant), b) *tanu* (weakened or attenuated), c) *vichinna* (intercepted), and d) *udara* (fully active or aroused).
Klishta:	Afflicted, hindered.
Kosha:	*Koshas* are the five sheaths that cover the overall human system. These are the 1) *annamaya kosha* (Food Sheath), 2) *pranamaya kosha* (pranic sheath), 3) *manomaya kosha* (mental sheath), 4) *vijnanamaya kosha* (intellectual sheath) and 5) *anandamaya kosha* (blissful sheath).
Krishna:	The last incarnation of God who appeared on earth over 5200 years ago. The speaker of the *Bhagavad Gita*. The primary form of God to be worshipped in this age.
Kriya:	*Kriyas* are classical Yoga techniques aimed at inner purification. This provides a cleansing process of one's inner body that results in high er knowledge and state of consciousness.
Krodha:	Anger, wrath, passion.
Kurukshetra:	(Lit. "the field of the Kurus") the setting of the *Bhagavad Gita*.
Maha Jagad Guru:	Great World Teacher.
Manas:	Mind. The storehouse of data, impressions, and memories.
Mandala:	Region.

Mantra: A Divine, liberating sound vibration.

Mantra-dhyana: *Mantra* meditation.

Maya: Illusion.

Moksha: Liberation, spiritual freedom.

Murti: Sacred image placed on altars and used in wor shipful meditation.

Namaste: "I offer my respects to you". A respectful greeting.

Narayana: A name of God. The "Sustainer of All Beings".

Narayana-mantra: Aum Namo Narayanaya. "I offer my respects to that Absolute Who is the sustainer of all be ings".

Niyama: Observances. One of the eight limbs of Yoga. The *niyamas* are 1) *shauca* (purity), 2) *santosha* (contentment), 3) *tapas* (austerity), 4) *svadhyaya* (self-study) and 5) *Ishvara-pranidhana* (devotion to Ishvara or God).

Paramatman: The supreme Self; the transcendental Self of our self; God.

Patañjali: The author of the *Yoga Sutras*.

Prakriti: Material nature. Prime matter. The power of creativity. One of God's energies.

Prana: Life energy, life force, or life current. These finer-than-atomic energies have inherent intelli- gence, as opposed to atoms and electrons, which are considered to be blind forces. The Chinese call this life force *chi*.

Pranayama: Yoga breathing exercises. *Pranayama* is one of the eight limbs of Yoga.

Pratyahara:	Withdrawing the senses in order to still the mind in meditation. One of the eight limbs of Yoga.
Prasada:	"Grace". Food or other objects offered to God and thus sanctified.
Prema:	Divine love.
Puja:	Worship ceremony. A meditation ritual.
Purusha:	Pure consciousness, the seer or witness.
Rishi:	Seer, sage, perfected *yogi*, revealer of sacred texts.
Sadhana:	Spiritual practice or discipline.
Sadhaka:	One who performs *sadhana*.
Samadhi:	Absorption of our consciousness in God, unitive awareness, the eighth limb of Yoga.
Samsara:	The wheel of material existence. The cycle of birth and death.
Samskara:	Stored impression or tendency of past action. An embodied memory.
Sanatana Dharma:	The Eternal Natural Way. The true name of the spiritual tradition commonly mislabeled "Hinduism".
Sankalpa:	Formative will; determination.
Santosha:	Contentment. One of the five *niyamas*.
Sat-sangha:	True/Good association.
Sattva:	Goodness, illumination, lightness, one of the three *gunas*.

Satya: Truthfulness, one of the five *yamas* (abstinences) of Yoga.

Seva: Service/voluntary action performed in devotion to God.

Shakti-da: Spiritual empowerment transmitted by God or by the *guru*.

Shanti: Peace.

Shastra: Scripture.

Shauca: Purity, one of the five *niyamas* (observances) of Yoga.

Shishya: Initiated student.

Shriman-Narayana: The highest name of God in Sanatana Dharma. It denotes both the male and female aspects of God together – Mother-Father God in the form of Sri Lakshmi and Narayana.

Siddhi: A perfection, or mystic power.

Sukha: Happiness, pleasure.

Sukshma: Astral, subtle body. The psychic form.

Sundaram: Beautiful, noble.

Sutra: (Lit. "thread") brief statement or aphorism often used to convey Dharma philosophy in brevity of form.

Svadhyaya: Self-study, one of the five *niyamas* (observances) of Yoga.

Svarupa: (Lit. "own form") The *atman's* eternal, spiritual form.

Tamas: Heaviness, darkness, inertia, ignorance. One of the three *gunas*.

Tapas:	Austerity, asceticism, challenging oneself. One of the five *niyamas* of Yoga.
Tattva:	Literally "that-ness", essence, a metaphysical Real in the Aristotelian sense.
Trataka:	A meditation consisting of gazing at a particular spot or flame.
Trikala-jnana:	Knowledge of the past, present, and future.
Trishna:	Craving, thirst.
Tri-Tattva:	The "Three Reals": the Absolute (Brahman), Materiality (Jagat), and the finite self (Atman).
Tulasi:	A plant that is very dear to Lord Krishna, and thus sacred.
Upadesha:	Sacred teachings.
Upanishads:	Ancient Vedic philosophical scriptures. There are 108 *Upanishads* in total.
Vasana:	Stored trait or tendency of past action.
Veda(s):	"Knowledge". The sacred scriptures (*Sha stras*) of Sanatana Dharma.
Vidya:	Wisdom, science, knowledge.
Virodha-vardhana-vada:	Marxism. The "Theory of Growth through Conflict". A Sanskrit term that I originated to describe this metaphysical theory.
Viveka:	Discrimination, discernment.
Vritti:	Fluctuation(s) of the *chitta* (mind-substance).
Vairagya:	Detachment.

Vedanta: Philosophical school propounded by Bada rayana Vyasa. It contains the teachings of the *Upanishads* and investigates the nature and rela tionship of the three Reals (Tri-tattva): the Ab solute (Brahman), Materiality (Jagat), and the finite self (Atman).

Yagna: Fire ceremony.

Yama: Restraint. One of the eight limbs of Yoga

Yamas & Niyamas: The ten ethical principles of Dharma.

Yoga: "Union". The systematic path, discipline, and philosophy for self-realization and God-consciousness.

Bibliography - Primary Sources

Anselm, St. *Proslogium.* Trans. S.N. Deane. 2nd ed. La Salle, IL: Open Court Publishing Company, 1962.

Baladeva Vidyabhushana. *The Vedanta-Sutras of Badarayana.* Trans. Rai Bhadur shrisa Chandra Vasu. 2nd ed. New Delhi: Munshiram Manoharlal Publishers, 1979.

The Bhagavad Gita. Trans. Deutsch, Eliot. New York: Holt, Rinehart and Winston, 1968.

Dharmaraja. *Vedantaparibhasha of Dharmaraja.* Sastri ed. and trans. S. S. Suryanarayana. Adyar: Adyar Library, 1942.

Gaudapada. *Mandukyopanishad with Gaudapada's Karika and Shankara's Commentary,* 4th ed., trans. Swami Nikhilananda. Mysore: Ra makrishna Ashram, 1955.

Gautama. *Gautama's Nyayasutras with Vatsyayana Bhashya,* Sanskrit ed. and English trans. Ganganatha Jha, 2 vols. Poona: Oriental Book Depot, 1939.

-----. *The Nyaya-Sutras of Gautama.* Trans. Gangunath Jha. 5 Vols. Delhi: Motilal Banarsidass, 1984.

Harsha. *Sri Harsha's* Khandanakhandakhadya. Trans. Phyllis Granoff. Dodrecht, Holland: D. Reidel Publishing Co., 1978.

Ishvarakrishna. Samkhyakarika, 4th ed., trans. S. S. Suryanarayana Sastri. Madras: University of Madras, 1948.

Jaimini. *Jaimini's Mimamsasutra with Shabara's Commentary and Notes,* trans. Ganganatha Jha, 3 vols., Gaekwad Oriental Series, Baroda: 1933-36; reprint Oriental Institute, 1973-1974.

Jiva Gosvamin. *Jiva Gosvamin's Tattvasandarbha.* Trans. Stuart Mark Elk man. Delhi: Motilal Banarsidass, 1986.

-----. *Sri Tattva-Sandarbha.* Trans. and Commmentary Satya Narayana

248

Dasa and Kundali Dasa. New Delhi: Jivas, 1995.

-----. *Bhagavatsandarbha.* Notes Chinmayi Chatterjee. Calcutta: Jadavpur University, 1972. Kancha.

Vaisheshikasutras of Kanada, trans. N. Sinha. Allahabad: Panini Office, 1911.

Keshava Mishra. *Tarkabhashyaa of Keshava Mishra,* 2nd ed., ed. and trans. G. Jha. Poona: Oriental Book Agency, 1949.

Krishnadasa Kaviraja Gosvamin. *Caitanyacaritamrita of Krishnadasa Gosva mi.* (ed. and trans., 2nd ed.). London: 1922.

Krishna Yajvan. *Mimamsaparibhasha of Krishna Yajvan,* ed. and trans. Swami Madhavanand. Belur Math: The Ramakrishna Mission Sarada Pitha, 1948.

Kumarila Bhatta. *Shlokavartika of Kumarila Bhatta with the Commentary of Nyayaratnakara of Parthasarathi Mishra,* trans. Ganganatha Jha (Cal cutta: Asiatic Society, 1907), ed. Swami Drankasa Sastri (Banaras: Tara Publications, 1978).

Madhva. *Anubhashya of Madhva.* Bombay: Nirnaya Sagara Press, S. S. Rao, trans., 2nd ed. Tirupati, 1936.

-----. *Madhva Brahmasutrabhashya with Several Commentaries,* 4 vols. R. Rag havacendra (ed.). Mysore: Government Branch Press, 1922.

-----. *Madhva's Commentary on the Brahmasutras.* (Trans. S. S. Rau) Madras: Thompson and Co., 1904.

Madhava Acharya. *The Sarva-Darshana-Samgraha.* Trans. E.B. Cowell and A.E. Gough. The Showkhamba Sanskrit Studies, Vol X. Vara nasi, India: Chowkhamba Sanskrit Series Office, 1978.

Manikana, A Navya-Nyaya Manual, ed. and trans. E. R. Sreekrishna Sarma. Adyar: Adyar Library, 1960.

Nimbarka. *Vedanta Parijata Saurabha and Vedanta Kausthubha of Shrinivasa,* trans. R. Bose. 3 vols. Calcutta: Royal Asiatic Soceity of Ben gal, 1940-43.

Panini. *Panini's Ashtadhayi*, ed. and trans. Shrisa Candra Vasu, 2 vols. Reprint Delhi: Motilal Banarsidass, 1961.

Patañjali. *Patañjali Mahabhashya*, ed. Vedavrata Snataka, 10 vols. Gurukul Jhajjar (Rohtak): Haryana Sahitya Samsthan, 1961-1964.

-----. *Patañjali's Yogasutra*, ed. and trans. Swami Vijnana Asrama. Ajmer: Sri Madanlal Laksminivas Chandak, 1961.

-----. *The Yoga-Sûtra of Patanjali: A New Translation and Commentary*, Inner Traditions International; Rochester, Vermont, 1989.

Ramanuja. *Sri-Bhashya*. Trans. Swami Vireswarananda and Swami Adidevananda. 2nd ed. Calcutta: Advaita Ashrama, 1986.

-----. *The Vedanta-Sutras with the Sri-Bhashya of Ramanujacharya*, Vol. I. Madras: The Educational Publishing Co., 1961.

-----. *Vedartha-Sangraha*. Trans. S. S. Raghavachar. Mysore: Sri Ramakrishna Ashrama, 1978.

Ramayaaa, Critical Edition, 7 vols. Baroda: Oriental Institute, 1960-1975.

Shabara. *Shabarabhashya*, with contemporary Sanskrit commentary by B. G. Apte, 6 vols. Poona: Anandashrama, 1931-1934. English trans. G. Jha, 3 vols. Baroda: Oriental Institute, 1973-1974.

Shankaracharya. *Aparokokshanubhuti of Shankaracharya*, trans. Swami Vimuktananda, 2nd ed. Calcutta: Ramakrishna Math, 1955.

-----. *Atmabodha*. Trans. Nikhilananda, Swami. Mylapore, Madras: Sri Ramakrishna Math, 1947.

-----. *Brahma-Sutra-Bhashya*. Trans. Swami Gambhirananda. Calcutta: Advaita Ashrama, 1983.

-----. *Eight Upanisads with the Commentary of Shankaracharya*. Trans. Swami Gambhirananda. 2 Vols. Calcutta: Advaita Ashrama, 1965.

-----. *Upadesha Sahasri of Sri Shankaracharya ("A Thousand Teachings")*. Trans. Mylapore, Madras: Sri Ramakrishna Math, 1961.

-----. *Minor Works of Sri Shankaracharya*, 2nd ed. Bhavagat, H. R. (ed.). Poona Oriental Series No. 8. Poona: Oriental Books Agency, 1952.

-----. *Vivekacudamani of Shankaracharya*, 7th ed., ed. And trans. Swami Madhavananda. Calcutta: Ramakrishna Math, 1966.

Shayana. *Rgveda with the Commentary of Shayana*, 2nd ed., 4 vols. Max Muller (ed.). London: 1892; reprint: Banaras: Chowkhambha Sanskrit Office, 1966.

Shripati. *Shripati's Shrikara Bhashya*, ed. Hayavadana Rao. Bangalore: 1936.

Srinivasadasa. *Yatindramadipika of Srinivasadasa*. Trans. Adidevananda, Swami. Madras: Sri Ramakrishna Math, Mylapore 1949.

Sureshvara. *The Naishkarmya Siddhi of Sri Sureshvara*. Trans. Alston, A.J. London: Shanti Sadan, 1959.

-----. *The Sambandha-Vartika of Sureshvaracharya*. Trans. Mahadevan, Swami. Madras: University of Madras, 1958.

Svatmarama Yogindra. *Hathayogapradipika by Svatmarama Yogindra*, 2nd ed., trans. Srinivasa Iyengar. Adyar: Theosophical Publishing House, 1933.

Tagare, Ganesh Vasudeo. *The Bhagavata-Purana*. 5 Vols. Dehli: Motilal Banarsidass, 1976.

Tapasyananda, Swami. *Srimad Bhagavata: The Holy Book of God*. Vols. 1-4. Madras: All India Press, 1982.

Udayana. *Nyayakrishnamanjali of Udayana*, ed. and trans. E. G. Cowell. Calcutta: 1864.

Upanishads. One Hundred and Eight Upanishads, 4th ed. W. C. Pancikar (ed.). Bombay: Nirnaya Sagar Press, 1932.

Vadiraja. *Vadiraja's Refutation of Shankara's Non-Dualism: Clearing the Way for Theism*. Trans. Betty, L. Stafford. Delhi: Motilal Banarsidass,

1978.

Vacaspati Mishra. *Nyayavartikatparyantika*. Ed. G. S. Tailanga. Viziana gram Sanskrit Series, no. 9, 1896.

-----. *The Bhamati of Vacaspati on Shankara's Brahmasutrabhashya*, ed. and trans. S. S. Suryanarayana Sastri and C. Kunhan Raja. Adyar: Theosophical Publishing House, 1933.

Vedanta Deshika. *Pañcaratra Raksha of Sri Vedanta Deshika*, critical eds. M. Duraiswami Aiyanjar and T. Venugopalacharya, with notes and variant readings, introduction by G. Srinivasa Murti. Adyar: Adyar Library, 1942.

Venkatacarya. *Vedantakarikavali of Venkatacharya*, ed. and trans. V. Krisna macarya. Adyar: Adyar Library, 1950.

Vishnu-purana, trans. H. H. Wilson. Reprint Calcutta: Punthi Pustak, 1961.

Bibliography - Secondary Sources

Adler, Mortimer J. "The Nature of Natural Law."
  http://radicalacademy.com/adlernaturallaw.htm.

Agarwal, Vishal. *The Ancient Commentators of Prasthana Trayi.* Unpublished
  manuscript,1998.

Balasubramanian, R. *Advaita Vedanta.* Madras: University of Madras,
  1976.

-----. "Advaita: An Overview." *Perspective of Theism and Absolutism in In
  dian Philosophy.* Ed. T.N. Ganapathy. Madras: Vivekananda Col
  lege, 1978.

Banerjee, N. V. *The Spirit of Indian Philosophy.* New Delhi: Arnold-
  Heinemann, 1958.

Barua, B. M. *History of Pre-Buddhistic Indian Philosophy.* Calcutta: Calcutta
  University, 1921.

Bharadwaj, K. D. *The Philosophy of Ramanuja.* New Delhi: Sir Sankar Lall
  Charitable Trust Society, 1958.

Burlamaqui, Jean-Jacques. *The Principles of Natural Law.* General Books,
  LLC, 2007.

Carman, J. B. *The Theology of Ramanuja: An Essay in Interreligious Understand
  ing.* New Haven, Conn., and London: Yale University Press,
  1974.

Chaudhuri, Roma. *Ten Schools of the Vedanta.* 3 vols. Calcutta: Rabindra
  Bharati University, 1981.

Coomaraswamy, Ananda. *Hinduism And Buddhism,* (Kessinger Publishing,
  2007)

----. *Spiritual Authority and Temporal Power in the Indian Theory of Government,*
  (Oxford University Press, 1994)

----. *What is Civilisation? and Other Essays.* (Oxford University Press, 1991)

Clooney, Francis X. *Thinking Ritually: Rediscovering the Purva Mimamsa of Jaimini*. Vienna, De Nobili Research Library, 1990.

Devi, Savitri. *A Warning to the Hindus*. Promilla Paperbacks, 1993.

Eliade, Mircea. *Yoga: Immortality and Freedom*. Princeton, NJ: Princeton University Press, 2009.

Evola, Julius. *Heathen Imperialism*. Thompkins & Cariou, 2007.

----. *Metaphysics of War: Battle, Victory and Death in the World of Tradition*. Ed. John Morgan. London: Arktos, 2007.

----. *Revolt Against the Modern World*. Inner Traditions, 1995.

Feuerstein, Georg. *Philosophy of Classical Yoga*. Inner Traditions, 1996.

----. *The Yoga Tradition: Its History, Literature, Philosophy and Practice*. Hohm Press (2001)

Frawley, David. *Arise Arjuna: Hinduism and the Modern World*. 1995.

----. *Gods, Sages, and Kings*, Lotus Press, Twin Lakes, Wisconsin.

----. *From the River of Heaven*, Lotus Press, Twin Lakes, Wisconsin.

----. *Hinduism and the Clash of Civilizations*. Voice of India, 2001.

----. *Universal Hinduism: Towards a New Vision of Sanatana Dharma*. Voice of India, 2010.

----. *Yoga and Ayurveda*, Lotus Press, Twin Lakes, Wisconsin.

Guénon, Réné. *Introduction to the Study of the Hindu Doctrines (Introduction générale à l'étude des doctrines hindoues*, 1921). Sophia Perennis, 2004.

----. *Man and His Becoming according to the Vedânta (L'homme et son devenir selon le Vêdânta*. Sophia Perennis, 2004.

----. *The Crisis of the Modern World (La crise du monde moderne*, 1927). Sophia Perennis, 2007.

----. *The King of the World*, Collected Works of Réné Guénon. Ghent, New York: Sophia Perennis, undated (originally published 1927)

----. *The Reign of Quantity & the Signs of the Times (Le règne de la quantité et les signes des temps*, 1945). Sophia Perennis, 2004.

Kak, Subhash. "The Assault on Tradition". Vigil, January, 2005.

Lehmann, Jean-Pierre. "The Dangers of Monotheism in the Age of Glo
   balization". The Globalist Magazine, March 30, 2006.

Prabhupada, A.C. Bhaktivedanta Swami. *Bhagavad-Gita As It Is* (1968).

----. *Dharma: The Way of Transcendence.* Bhaktivedanta Book Trust, 1998.

----. *Easy Journey to Other Planets.* Bhaktivedanta Book Trust, 1970.

----. *Srimad-Bhagavatam* (30 Vols.). Bhaktivedanta Book Trust, 1972–77.

----. *The Science of Self-Realization* Bhaktivedanta Book Trust, 1977.

Rothbard, N. Murray. *The Ethics of Liberty.* NYU Press, 2003

Saint-Yves d'Alveydre, Alexandre. *Mission de l'Inde en Europe.* University
   of Michigan Library, 1910.

Schall, James Vincent. "Natural Law and Economics," *Religion & Liberty*,
   3 (May/June, 1993), 3-6.

Scruton, Roger. *Culture Counts: Faith and Feeling in a World Besieged.* En
   counter Books, 2007.

----. *The Aesthetic Understanding.* St. Augustines Press; 2nd edition, No
   vember, 1998.

Spengler, Oswald. *Der Untergang des Abendlandes (The Decline of the West).*
   Vol. 1&2. General Books, 2010.

About Sri Acharyaji

Sri Dharma Pravartaka Acharya is universally acclaimed as one of the world's most respected and qualified Dharma teachers and leaders. Dr. Deepak Chopra exclaimed about Sri Acharyaji in 2002: "*You've done truly phenomenal work teaching the pure essence of Yoga*". In a similar manner, Dr. David Frawley has said about Sri Acharyaji, "*Sri Acharyaji represents the Sankalpa [the will] of the Hindu people and the cause of Sanatana Dharma. I urge all Hindus everywhere to give him your full support, assistance, and encouragement in his crucial work. He needs and deserves our help.*" Sri Acharyaji has the support and encouragement of many hundreds of the world's most respected Vedic *guru*, leaders and teachers.

Sri Acharyaji began his personal spiritual journey over 40 years ago at the tender age of ten when he read the *Bhagavad Gita* for the very first time. He then spent many years in intensely dedicated spiritual practice, living as a celibate monk for over six years. He took brahamana (priest) initiation directly from his guru, Bhakti Rakshaka Sridhara Swami, in 1986.

He coupled his decades of intense spiritual practice and study with advanced academic achievements, earning a B.A. in philosophy/theology from Loyola University Chicago, as well as an M.A. and Ph.D. in religious studies from the University of Wisconsin-Madison.

Explaining to his doctoral advisor that "*I don't want to just study the history of religion…I want to make religious history*", Sri Acharyaji eventually left academia to devote himself exclusively to spiritual teaching and to the preservation of the great tradition of Sanatana Dharma.

Following the order that his guru gave him in 1986 to become an American guru, Sri Acharyaji finally began acting in the role of an official guru in 1998. It was at this time that he founded the International Sanatana Dharma Society.

Sri Acharyaji was the Resident Acharya (Spiritual Preceptor) of the Hindu Temple of Nebraska from 2007-2009, which represents the first time in American history that a Hindu temple had ever made such an esteemed appointment.

Today, Sri Acharyaji occupies his full time teaching Dharma spirituality to diverse audiences. In addition to leading classes, *satsanghas*, seminars and lecturing on Sanatana Dharma widely, Sri Acharyaji is a renowned author, as well as a personal spiritual guide (*guru*) to a rapidly increasing following of enthusiastic students from both the Indian and the non-Indian communities.

He is the current President and Acharya of the non-profit spiritual movement known as the International Sanatana Dharma Society.

For more information about the life and teachings of Sri Dharma Pravartaka Acharya, please visit his website: www.dharmacentral.com

CPSIA information can be obtained
at www.ICGtesting.com
Printed in the USA
LVHW030436091122
732724LV00030B/1333